Melody for Nora

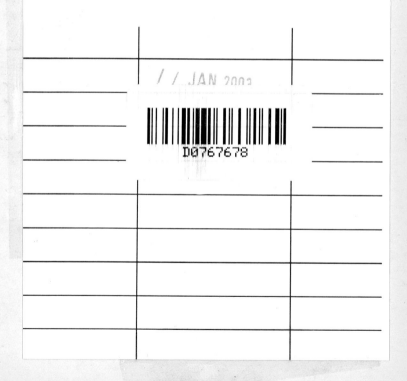

/ / JAN 2003

D0767678

For Joan, Jane and Ruth

Melody for Nora

MARK O'SULLIVAN

WOLFHOUND PRESS

Reprinted 1995
First published 1994 by
WOLFHOUND PRESS Ltd
68 Mountjoy Square
Dublin 1

© 1994 Mark O'Sullivan

Wolfhound Press receives financial assistance from the Arts Council/An Chomhairle Ealaíon, Dublin.

British Library Cataloguing in Publication Data
O'Sullivan, Mark
    Melody for Nora
    I. Title
    832.914 [J]

ISBN 0-86327-425-0

Cover illustration: Katharine White
Cover design: Joe Gervin
Typesetting: Wolfhound Press
Printed by the Guernsey Press Co Ltd, Guernsey, Channel Isles.

When we dream
we make fantastic stories
from the little details of our lives.

In these pages I've done the same
with some of the details of
my grandmother's and my grandaunt's early lives.

I thank them for having lived
and given me the chance to dream.

It was the summer of 1922. The war of Independence had ended when General Michael Collins signed a peace treaty the previous year. Ireland was at last free — but at the cost of being divided.

People were glad to see the Irish army replace the hated Black and Tans, who were said to have been drawn from the ranks of criminals and thugs. The British Secret Service withdrew from their base at Dublin Castle. The days of assassinations and terror seemed over.

But some rejected the terms of the peace treaty, and refused to recognise the new Irish Free State. They took up arms against the new government and its Regular army, forming a force known as the Irregulars.

When these men attacked the Four Courts building in Dublin's city centre, the first shots of the Irish Civil War were fired. A new and bitter conflict had begun . . .

Chapter 1

It was like no room she had ever been in before. Her eyes ached in the intense light. Around her there were no walls, only masses of white billowing curtains tossed by the winds of some eternity.

The piano at which she sat was equally unfamiliar. Its keys were not stained or yellowed. They gleamed so brightly that it was hard to tell where one note ended and the next began.

Strangest of all was the piece she played and how easily, how faultlessly she played it. She was certain she had never heard it before and each turn it took was a further step into a landscape of new discovery.

Even as she played, Nora was convinced that she had only imagined that her mother and father and the two boys had ever existed. Where she had come from and where she was going she had no idea. She was sure of one thing only, that close behind her someone was standing, watching, listening.

The intruder could not be Mrs Teehan, her piano teacher, because she had never feared her. Neither could it be, with his precise little voice, the long-nosed examiner who had tested her last month. It was certainly a man but one she had never met. This stranger was, she knew, a young man made old by the sorrows of life. He might be cruel or kind or both. She struggled to decide whether to turn and tell him to go away or continue with her melody to see how it ended.

Then, before her very eyes, her fingers began to bleed as she played. There was no pain, no letting up in the pace of the waltz. Nothing but sheer terror. When she turned to the stranger for help, he was gone.

As she ran towards the spot where he'd stood she heard a dull thud. Looking back she saw that the lid of the piano had slammed shut. She searched desperately for a window or a door to escape through but the room was closing in on her. The flowing curtains entangled her like a vast spider's web.

Her hand fell blindly on cold, polished timber and she pushed it away. The piano went sliding across the floor and crashed with an almighty bang through the stifling lace and away into whatever lay beyond . . .

~

Nora woke with a start and heard in the distance another huge crash, echoing too often to be a real echo. Rubbing the sleep out of her eyes the reality of what was happening dawned on her. Those men and women who had fought side by side for their country's freedom would turn their venom and their hatred on one another. The Civil War feared by so many had begun.

For months now the two sides had been drawing closer and closer to conflict. Down at the Four Courts where the Irregulars had moved in to defy the new Government, the atmosphere bristled with tension. Last month there had been an election and the people had voted for the Treaty and for peace. But the Irregulars were unmoved.

'The world is full,' her mother had said, 'of people who think they know what's best for everyone else.'

Nora Canavan looked across to where her twin brothers slept on undisturbed. Even in this faint light there was no doubt of their existence. Snuggled up together, their faces were as full of mischief as when they were awake. She wondered if the feud waking the city that night would still be blazing when the boys reached fighting age, whatever that might be. Eighteen, probably. That was ten years away. She had read in school of a Twenty Years War, and more chillingly still of the Hundred Years War. She shivered to think that there might be nights like this for as long as she lived — if she survived the bombs and bullets of those who knew best.

From her mother's room she heard a sudden movement and held her breath to listen. There was silence followed by more heavy fire from the city centre. She tried to find some rhythm in the distant thundering but there was none. Then came two weak knocks on the wall above her head. It was her mother's call.

Nora slipped quietly out of bed and as she brushed by them, the boys turned over together as if dreaming the same dream. Standing in her mother's doorway she was struck once again by the unmistakable odour of sickness. No matter how long she spent scrubbing the floor in there, no matter how long the window was left open, the foulness remained elusive. Nora squinted hard to trace the outline of a face on a sunken pillow.

'Nora, love,' her mother whispered, 'are ye all right out there?'

'We're fine.'

'The guns are started and there's no sign of your father.'

Nora went to her mother's side and held her cold, damp hands in hers.

'You know where he'll be,' she said.

At fourteen Nora was still too ashamed of hating her father to let it show. She still imagined it must be her fault as much as his that they regarded each other with such contempt.

'I don't know,' her mother said. 'A night like this anything might happen to him!'

'He'll be fine,' Nora assured her, pushing to the back of her mind the guilty hope that something might indeed happen to him. She was certain he was in the same place where he spent every other night. For him she was sure, the bombs at the Four Courts would be the excuse for an extra drink or two.

'But he's an awful impulsive man,' her mother worried.

It was beyond Nora's understanding that her mother had even an ounce of feeling left for this man who had made their lives so miserable. Since she'd become unwell her concern for him had grown as surely as his seemed to fade. He never tried to make things easier for her. When she took one of those awful dizzy spells he would simply leave Nora to deal with her, and with her crying, confused brothers.

On the window-sill a little oblong box containing her mother's small savings tinkled as another shell went off. The flash lit up their faces. Nora clasped her hands tighter.

'Don't be afraid, girl. There'll be no fighting up here.'

Nora remembered that evening last week when her mother had begun to talk vaguely about a future where she might no longer be around. It came as such a shock that Nora felt, for the first time since the illness had started, a terrible resentment towards her. She shouted at her, blaming her for letting herself waste away and not trying to get well. Her mother had said nothing and waited for the bitterness to fade in the comfort of her touch. Now it was Nora's turn to offer reassurance.

'I'll go down and make sure the door isn't bolted,' she said.

By now, Nora's eyes had grown accustomed to the darkness and she made her way quickly down the narrow stairway. At the foot of the stairs she heard her father's snoring. She found him stretched out on the old, patched-up sofa, his head back and his mouth open. For a moment his snoring stopped and she imagined he was dead. Angry with herself for thinking like this and with him for worrying her mother, she grabbed his shoulder and shook it roughly. He threw out his arm in fright and his hand caught her on the cheek.

'Jumpin' Jehosepheth!' he muttered, peering madly about the room.

'You hit me!' Nora cried trying to keep her trembling voice down.

'What're you talking about? I never even saw you,' he shouted.

The reek of whiskey filled her nostrils. She swallowed hard. If she protested any more he would fly into a rage and the whole house would be in turmoil.

'Don't shout or you'll wake the lads.'

He dragged himself upright and Nora backed away into the shadows.

'Answering back again, you little ...' he roared but before he could lunge at her the guns started up again.

'God almighty,' he said, 'will they ever stop fighting over this rotten little country?'

He collapsed on to the sofa again and stared into the embers in the fireplace. Nora wasn't yet sure if it was safe to sneak out of the room. She knew he hadn't meant to hit her this time. Her cheek stung but it was her feelings that were really hurt. She wished he'd say he was sorry. Just this once.

'They won't be happy 'til they blow us all to smithereens for the glory of Ireland,' he complained to no-one in particular.

'Mam's waiting for you above,' Nora told him.

'Get up to bed and don't be annoying me head!' he blurted out. 'You're nothing only a troublemaker.'

Nora knew what would come next. It was always the same when he came back from the pub. His anger would be turned on her because he had decided she was to blame for her mother's condition.

'Only for you and your damned music that woman would be as healthy as ... as ...' he began to sniffle drunkenly.

It was better, she thought, to stay quiet and let him repeat his accusations against her. Silently she squeezed her fingers together, thinking of how her hands had bled in her dream, the hands that were to blame for all of this. She wished she could break each finger one by one or that like the lepers she learned about in school she would wake some morning and find they had fallen from her hand.

Three years ago her mother had taken her to the comfortable red-brick house on the South Circular Road where Mrs Margaret Teehan lived. It was Nora's eleventh birthday and the truth was it had been a disappointing day. Already late evening, there had been no present from her mother. No matter how bad things were she had always come up with some little gift. Now, however, as they walked along Clanbrassil Street she wondered if her mother had found something in one of the pawn shops and her excitement grew.

'Where are we going, Mam?' she questioned as they turned the corner on to the South Circular Road.

'You'll soon see,' was all her mother would say.

Nora wanted to scream or at least let some of the tears that had been welling up all day flow down her unhappy face.

'But, Mam!' she cried when they stopped at Mrs Teehan's door, 'We don't know anybody over here.'

Her mother fixed up Nora's hair and checked her hands again to make sure for the umpteenth time they were clean.

The sight which greeted Mrs Teehan was for her an unfamiliar one. This was the time of year when the well-dressed wives of merchants and bankers and the like brought their darling and usually reluctant little brats to begin or resume their piano lessons. Nora and her mother were not dressed in rags but their clothes showed the signs of too much wear and meticulous cleaning. Their cuffs were threadbare and there was the odd, unmatched button.

'Mrs Canavan, is it?' Mrs Teehan smiled and Nora decided right away that she liked the red-cheeked, slightly dumpy woman.

'I hope we're not late,' Mrs Canavan said shyly.

Mrs Teehan was relieved not to be addressed in the usual haughty manner of her more typical customers.

'And this must be Nora, our new pupil.'

'But I have a school, Mam!'

Then everything was explained. Her birthday present was to learn to play the piano. Nora was overwhelmed. There had never been any mention of such a thing before. No talk of music at all, though she sang all the time around the house, just like her mother. She wasn't sure if this was something she really wanted to do. Her mother looked so perfectly happy sipping tea in Mrs Teehan's parlour, however, that she felt it must be right for her.

For weeks Nora fumbled her way awkwardly through the lessons. She tried not to seem ungrateful but couldn't help complaining to her mother. Mrs Teehan also wondered if the girl would ever do more than plod through the scales in her heavy-handed way. Nora's hands were not the delicate kind you might have expected to float lightly along the keyboard. They were far from fragile and too familiar with hard work.

Mrs Teehan decided to let Nora's mother know, in the nicest possible way, that perhaps this was not such a good idea after all. She had many plodders in the ranks of her pupils but she knew their parents could well afford to fritter away money on them. It was obvious that Mrs Canavan had better things to spend it on. However, before she brought herself to do this, a remarkable change came about.

It began when they moved from the chore of scales to the first simple piece of music. The stiffness seemed to leave Nora's fingers and slowly an unexpected grace entered them. From that point on Nora's talent blossomed until now, three years later, she was beyond doubt the most gifted pupil Mrs Teehan had ever taught. Her confidence grew as she took each exam in her stride and her mother and teacher made plans for her future. Then, her mother fell ill and dreams began to fade.

That was when her father began to blame Nora. There had been many nights like this one, the night guns began to blaze down at the Four Courts. Always it came back to the same cruel accusation.

Her mother had taken a cleaning job in Capel Street to pay for Nora's lessons. Every Saturday evening she went there and Nora's father was convinced that this was the cause of her sickness. Nora came to believe it too despite her mother's protestations.

As she stood in the dark kitchen Nora's heart filled with hatred for her father and for music and, most of all, for herself. She waited for him to hit her again, certain she deserved it but he fell asleep on the sofa. She went to tell her mother he was home and everything was all right.

Difficult as it was to imagine an end to the battle raging in the city centre, it was even more impossible to imagine a time when her own life would change. It would take an eternity, she thought.

She was wrong. During the next two months her mother's condition worsened and there was to be no improvement. She died peacefully and, on an August morning in 1922, she was laid to rest.

Chapter 2

The young priest rushing through the prayers at Mrs Canavan's graveside felt a twinge of guilt. Like most of those present his mind was preoccupied with another death — one they could not help thinking was infinitely more important than this sadness in the hearts of the Canavans.

It was cold for the time of year and dark for the time of day. On the other side of the Liffey the streets of Dublin were too crowded, and the crowds were too quiet. Two days ago, history had taken a wrong turning and now it lurched away in its mistaken direction as surely as the funeral procession headed for Glasnevin Cemetery.

Along the six-mile route every vantage point was taken up. Every last square inch of pavement was filled with grieving people. Men dropped on one knee as the cortège passed and teardrops escaped the corners of many eyes. The horses drawing the funeral carriage banged their iron hooves on the cobblestones.

Their leader was dead. Michael Collins. Murdered not by

the Black 'n' Tans or the old British Secret Service from the
Castle but by one of his own countrymen. His death had left
a stain on every soul. Even his worst enemies knew in their
hearts that no good would come of it. People from both sides
no less than those who took no side wondered how long the
madness of Civil War would now prevail.

Inside the gates of Glasnevin Cemetery the atmosphere
reached its darkest depths in the hushed cacophony of the
last prayers. Soon the people moved away, as if every last one
of them was in a trance that might never be broken.

Far from these mourning crowds, the small group left
behind in that other cemetery began to move reluctantly from
the newly-filled grave.

Nora walked between her brothers, her arms holding them
comfortingly. Her mad shock of fair, strawy hair was for once
tied back and she wore her best Sunday dress. She looked
older than her fourteen years. Her face was care-worn from
the months of watching her mother die and worry over what
was to happen next. There seemed only one answer to that
question. She would have to become a mother to the boys.

By now she had almost grown used to the idea. Her mother
had been able to do very little these past few months. Washing and ironing, cooking and shopping had occupied Nora's
time, replacing the street games and easy friendships of other
girls. Still, it never occurred to her that it was at all unfair. It
was her duty.

Her father had already made it clear she wouldn't be
returning to school. This didn't surprise or bother her. The
fact was that most girls she knew were expected to go out and
get a job to help pay the family bills. She had not objected
either when he'd announced an end was to be put to her
piano lessons. Her only regret was that she would probably
never meet Mrs Teehan again. She had just said goodbye to

her at the graveyard and accepted this small loss which was trivial beside the heartache of losing her mother.

A few paces behind her came Mrs Rosie Tobin, their good friend and neighbour. She had seen them all through the worst of times. A widow herself she lived next door to the Canavans with her middle-aged son. She was smaller than Nora and thin as a rake. Her hair was dyed a strange, dark, unnatural brown. Some people thought her quite odd but Nora didn't care. She knew that without her they would never have survived these last few months.

Up ahead of Nora and her brothers walked Aunt Molly, her mother's sister, and Peter, her husband. Though they lived barely a hundred miles away she had never before seen them. Her mother rarely mentioned them and when she did she refused to answer Nora's questions about them. How could they come now that she was dead, and attempt to share in their grief when they had never bothered to come before? She looked at them with suspicion and not a little resentment.

Aunt Molly was, as Rosie Tobin whispered, 'grey as a badger'. Hair was of the utmost importance to Rosie! With her grey hair, her thick spectacles and a certain severity around the mouth she was totally unlike her dead sister. Nora wondered if they really were sisters knowing that in reality they might just as well not have been, so little did they ever see of each other.

As for Uncle Peter, he was tall and broad-shouldered and not in the least comfortable in his dark suit and tie. His hair was quite thin on top and he brushed it back constantly with his hand as if to assure himself it was still there.

'Bald as an egg before he's fifty! Wait 'til you see!' Rosie had pronounced gravely.

Molly and Peter quickened their pace and moved alongside Nora's father now. They seemed to have nothing to say to him. As bad as her father had been, Nora thought, he deserved better than their silence. Nora couldn't quite decide whether they could not or simply would not speak to him.

Back at their terraced railway house in Inchicore, Nora rushed about setting the table. A great unease was beginning to well up inside her. Every gesture she noticed added to her growing discomfort. Her father's impatient glances. Her aunt and uncle's eyes following her every move. The silence that fell on their efforts at conversation whenever she entered the room. It was no longer, she was sure, because they had nothing to talk about. Rather it was that the subject of their conversation was so difficult and painful.

'What are they talking about?' she asked in exasperation of Rosie.

'They're only being civil to each other,' she said. 'Small talk.'

'It's something to do with me, isn't it?'

'I'm sure they have better things to be gossiping about,' Rosie laughed. 'Put out those spoons on the saucers now and I'll bring in the tea.'

Just as she went to the door she heard her father sigh deeply and murmur: 'God almighty ... a man shouldn't have to do a thing like this!'

She dropped the spoons and they clattered in around the floor of the sitting room. Her father jumped to his feet and went towards her with a roar.

'Pick them up, you bloody eejit!'

As she stooped, she saw the white knuckles of his clenched fists. He moved a step closer but in a quiet, sudden instant her uncle was there between them and on his knees helping to find the spoons.

'I'll do it myself,' she said. 'It was my own fault.'

On her feet again she looked across at her father whose

eyes were closed tight as his fists had been a moment before.

'Nora,' he said softly and she waited. He said no more. She laid the spoons on the good china saucers and her heart had grown cold again as she said.

'Would you like to sit up to the table, Aunt Molly?'

'You're a great girl, do you know that,' her aunt said, her voice shaking in the tension-filled air.

Nora's smile was as false as the words she spoke to her father: 'Daddy, you could do with a cup of tea. Mrs Tobin made an iced cake for us.'

'Grand,' he said weakly, 'Grand,' and sat down heavily at the head of the table.

Mrs Tobin swept in with the teapot and jollied things along for a while through the awkwardness and hesitation that followed. Even Nora herself tried hard to keep the words flowing. Her father however was lost in thought and her aunt and uncle rarely took their eyes from him.

'Isn't it just as well yis came up last evening now all the same,' Rosie offered by way of another silence breaker.

'Why so, Mrs Tobin?' Peter asked.

'My fellow,' Rosie said, ('my fellow' being her son, she never called him anything else). 'My fellow says they blew up a bridge near Portarlington so the people couldn't make it up to the funeral above in Glasnevin.'

Molly moved her hand across the table and gripped her husband's shoulder.

'Aren't them Irregulars an awful shower. They've no respect for livin' nor dead,' Rosie added.

Nora was certain she detected a look of discomfort on her uncle's face. He fiddled with his stiff collar and said: 'War is a desperate thing the way it twists people's minds.'

'If you ask me, Mr Delaney,' Rosie told him, 'There's some minds are easy twisted!'

'I don't know but you're right there, Mrs Tobin,' he said despondently.

'Anyway,' she went on, 'my fellow says they'll have the line cleared this evening so you'll be all right for tomorrow.'

She had hardly finished speaking when Nora's father slammed his fist down on the table and stood up suddenly.

'I won't have it,' he said threateningly, his eyes fixed on Peter. 'I won't let this happen.'

'Jim,' Molly pleaded, 'we only ask you to consider what she wanted. God be good to her.'

'You're putting a gun to my head,' he shouted, 'D'ye think I have no heart just because ... just because ...'

He paused and looked at Nora. She was confused and thought grief must be driving him a little mad.

'Daddy, what are you saying?' she asked fearfully.

He didn't answer. Nora wished her mother was here to get the truth out of him. She could always do that. He made for the door and Nora guessed where he was going, where he always went when things got on top of him.

'Please stay here,' she pleaded quietly but he ignored her.

'I'll let you know in the morning,' he said to Peter and was gone.

Nora couldn't wait for her aunt and uncle to leave. Somehow, she felt, their presence held hidden dangers for her.

'We'd better get back to the hotel,' Molly said finally and they left with forlorn and worried smiles, 'We'll see you all tomorrow.'

That night Rosie got all of them to bed and in spite of their loneliness and sadness they slept. Nora and her brothers never heard their father come in from the pub or step falteringly up the stairs or stand, his eyes wet with tears, at their bedroom door. It was his first kindness to them in years not to wake them and they never knew.

Chapter 3

It was one of those days that begins dizzily and carries you along so quickly that nothing you do will make things stop happening. To begin with they all slept too soundly and but for Rosie's furious knocking might still have been in bed when Molly and Peter arrived. Nora rushed frantically to get the boys washed and dressed while Rosie went about organising the breakfast.

The boys rubbed their eyes and groaned, 'Why do we have to dress up fancy again?'

For them it was a real penance trying to keep their clothes clean all day when all they wanted to do was climb walls and jump in puddles. Nora wasn't sure either why they had to be shining again but their father insisted. In any case the boys were young enough not to be given reasons. Nora herself had grown used to not expecting reasons.

"Cause that's the why,' Nora told them, 'Now show me your hands.'

Only when the delicious smells from the frying pan rose

from the kitchen did the grumpy pair hurry themselves.

'Hey,' they both called out, 'It's Sunday again!'

They laughed excitedly and Nora wondered how they could behave as if their mother was downstairs waiting for them. She let them laugh because she knew that even if they'd forgotten for a brief while, they would remember soon enough.

'Sorry, Rosie,' she called as she ran down to the kitchen, 'We're terrible lazy!'

'If I could only sleep as well myself,' Rosie said, 'The way my fellow snores you'd want the Great Wall of China between the rooms to get a minute's rest!'

Nora tried to think of something to say that wouldn't sound ungrateful to Rosie for taking her mother's place in the kitchen.

'Thanks for coming,' was the best she could do.

'Go on out of that,' Rosie shrugged, 'Get the table ready there or they'll be in on top of us and nothing to shove in front of them only excuses.'

'I don't see why they have to come here again,' Nora grumbled, bothered by the mysterious talk of the previous afternoon.

'They're kith and kin, Nora!' Rosie chided, looking across at her, 'God, you're worse than my fellow's father. Every time my sainted mother used to call up he'd put down whatever class of a book he was reading and mutter, "Sacred Jaysus, what does she want comin' up here for?" '

Soon everything was ready and with perfect timing Molly and Peter knocked on the front door. Nora's father got up from his chair at the fire and cleared his throat. Nora looked in from the kitchen as he held his clenched fist to his chin and then straightened his fingers out and brushed them through his hair.

Finally, on the third knock, he thrust his hands forlornly into his pockets and went slowly to the door. His shoulders were more bent than usual. For some strange reason she thought of the Civil War again. She couldn't help feeling that this was what it looked like when people surrendered.

In the doorway Peter seemed to be asking something of her father who was nodding in agreement. Peter looked at her father gravely, held his arm for a moment and then let go.

There was little talk as they moved around the sitting room and found their places at the table. Even the boys were quiet, their minds firmly fixed on the feast to come.

'Two breakfasts in the one morning,' Peter exclaimed. 'There's times when I don't even get one!'

'A pity,' his wife joked, 'Your mother didn't show you how to make a cup of tea!'

Nora's father laughed but his lower lip trembled as he spoke.

'I couldn't make one myself. There's not much I can do,' he said. 'Only for Nora we'd be lost.'

Nora was surprised and embarrassed by this outburst. He went quiet again and they finished the meal quickly and uncomfortably. Rosie was about to begin clearing away the plates when Nora's father asked her to wait for a few minutes. They had something important to talk about.

'This is family business now,' Rosie objected, 'I should make myself scarce.'

'Would you stay,' her father asked, 'And tell me if I'm doing right?'

Nora grew pale with anxiety. The boys stared dumbly at their father. Under the table Nora took Rosie's hand and drew strength from it. She wished her aunt would stop looking at her with that sorrowful half-smile.

'Your mother,' Nora's father began, gazing over the heads

of his children, 'Your mother knew only too well that she might not get better, that we might be left on our own, the four of us.'

The boys began to whimper. Nora took her hand from Rosie's and held their small trembling frames.

'So she ... she made plans and I said there was no need for these at all, these plans ... but I see now, I know now she was right – like she always was,' he continued, smiling half-heartedly at Nora. 'And, well, she wrote to your aunt here and to my brother Phil in America, after we talked of course, and Molly was decent enough to say yes and my brother too wrote to say he'd be delighted to give the boys a chance in America ... And Nora, you'll be going down to Tipperary like Mam wanted for you.'

Tears began to trickle down his rough unshaven cheeks now and the boys were crying quietly too. They didn't yet understand what was happening and were more upset by the extraordinary sight of their father crying than anything else. Nora thought she might never breathe again. Her mouth hung open and her lungs ached for air.

'See, I wouldn't be able to manage and I couldn't hold down the job and look after the three of yis at the same time. I'd do it if I could but your mother was right about that too and I know in my heart and soul, I'd let ye down. I know that.'

Molly dabbed her eyes with her handkerchief. Her husband shook his head sympathetically. Nora struggled to speak.

'But we could make a go of it, Daddy!' she stuttered. 'I ... I'm done with school anyway, I'll have all the time in the world to ...'

'Nora,' her father interrupted, 'This is the hardest thing your mother ever asked me to do. God knows, I let her down often enough. I couldn't go back on my word to her.'

There seemed to be little left to say. Nora's father turned to Rosie and she nodded silently, giving her blessing to the plan. Nora wanted to protest longer and louder but she knew this would upset the boys even more. If Rosie agreed, she thought, it must be for the best. Still the feeling of emptiness inside her was vast as she tried to make sense of what her mother had done to the family. It was difficult not to believe that she had done something unforgivably cruel and wrong.

Her cheeks were burning now as she turned her resentment on her aunt and uncle. She wouldn't let them believe for one instant that she could ever be happy with them. At the back of her mind was a vague notion that if she behaved badly enough towards them they might eventually give up on her and send her back to her father. She could perhaps tell the boys to do the same with Uncle Phil in America.

'When will I have to go?' she asked of her father.

'There's a train in two hours, love,' Molly said, 'We were hoping to make that.'

'Don't call me love!' Nora snarled and stood up holding her brothers' hands.

'Where are you going?' her father demanded.

'I'm getting my things ready,' she snapped, 'The sooner I'm packed, the sooner I'll be out of your way!'

Her father didn't respond. She realised it was a waste of time being angry with him. The idea hadn't been his in the first place. Blaming him for everything that went wrong had become a habit that wasn't easily broken. Especially not at a time like this.

'I'll come with you, Nora,' Rosie said. 'We can sort out the boys' clothes while we're at it.'

Only now did she think of asking when they would be going.

'It'll be a month or two,' her father told her. 'Phil is to send the fare for their passage.'

He dragged himself to the front door and gazed out at the street that was always full of children but would soon be empty of his own.

It didn't take long for Nora to show Rosie which of the boys' clothes needed washing and which could be folded in readiness for their departure. It took even less time to gather her own few bits and pieces.

She thought about the many people she knew or heard about who'd gone to America. Few of them ever returned. She wondered what kind of man Uncle Phil was. She had only ever seen one old photograph of him. Would he treat the boys as if they were his own or would he make slaves of them? In the photograph he had looked a happy-go-lucky type of fellow. She hoped he still was.

As for her own destiny, Tipperary was just as strange and unknown a place to her as America was to the boys. She had never been there. If it meant anything to her it was the distant sadness that entered her mother's voice on those few occasions when she mentioned it. When she was younger it had never occurred to Nora to wonder why her mother never went back there even to visit or why her sister, Molly, never came to see her.

During the last few weeks these things had often come to mind but she knew the questions would be too painful for her mother to bear. Why should this uncaring couple now decide to carry out her final wish for Nora? And why did her mother want to send her to the very place that must have caused her so much grief? Why too had she not prepared her for this shock? Was it, perhaps, Nora's reaction when her mother first mentioned the prospect of her own passing?

'Rosie!' she pleaded hopelessly, 'I could mind the house and the boys and Daddy. I'm well able to, aren't I?'

'Better able than myself for it,' Rosie said. 'But your mother wants something more for you. A chance for you to do something with your life and your music and all.'

'That's what killed her Rosie. I might as well have strangled her with my bare hands.'

'You want to put that nonsense out of your head,' Rosie told her. 'The music kept your mother going. I'm telling you night, noon and morning I heard nothing else but how brilliant you were. I declare to God, it was worse than listening to my fellow boasting about his pigeons.'

Nora was grateful for Rosie's kindness but she wouldn't be persuaded from thinking as she did.

'Will you do something for me, Rosie?' she asked.

'And why wouldn't I!'

'The boys. Will you take them up to your house before I go? It'd be awful hard for them, saying goodbye and all.'

'You're like your mother, always thinking of everyone else,' Rosie said, gently touching her arm.

Nora moved away quickly to wrap her small bundle of clothes. She felt embarrassed and a little ashamed to be compared to her mother.

'No, I'm not!' she said and there was more than a hint of anger in her voice. 'I'm selfish, pure selfish.'

'That's not true,' Rosie said, 'And even if it was, I don't know but there's times when you have to be selfish and do what's best for yourself. Now, down with you and there's no need to say ...'

At the door Nora whispered over her shoulder:

'Goodbye, Rosie,' and ran down to where they waited for her. Rosie followed and called the boys.

'Who's going to come and clean out the pigeon loft for my fellow?'

The boys jumped at the chance since they knew this job

was worth at least a penny each to them. Nora turned away
as they went out the door with Rosie. Her father stared
helplessly after them. Nora could almost imagine forgiveness
was possible when he stood there so completely broken. In
an instant the spell was shattered however.

'What am I going to do without them little fellows?' he
said.

Nora's stomach sank. She noticed a flash of anger appear
on Molly's face but she didn't want her sympathy. Nora's
voice was edged with an icy bitterness.

'We'll be late for the train.'

She was gone through the door before any of them could
reply. Molly ran out after her.

'Nora, I know it's not easy for you but don't you want to
say something to your father?'

'No,' she said and just then he appeared at the door. He
was talking to Peter.

'I'll be sending the few bob every week, mind, to help with
her keep. Jimmer Casey, he's a workmate of mine, he's on
that run down to Tipperary these times. I'm sure he won't
mind dropping it down to you!'

'Fine,' Peter said. 'That'll be fine. Whatever you can manage.'

'Are you sure,' her father blurted out suddenly, 'things are
alright down there? Are they fighting below there? I mean,
are you sure it'll be safe for her?'

'There's nothing to worry about, Jim.' Molly assured him.
'We haven't had any bother. Sure haven't we half the Free
State Army below in the town!'

Nora was already walking away up the street with her
parcel of clothes under her arm. She realised with a sick
feeling that there were no friends she had to say goodbye to.
They had drifted away as she spent more and more time

working in the house. She quickened her pace afraid that at any moment the boys might run out on to the street and see her go. She couldn't bring herself to glance back at the house. There was, she felt sure, a curse on that place and if she was to look back she would be cursed too. Perhaps, she thought, she already was cursed.

'Bye, Nora,' her father called. She turned the corner and left his words to echo along the empty footpath and fade like the last wisp of love in her heart for him.

Chapter 4

Kingsbridge Railway Station was a familiar place to Nora. It was her father's workplace. Her mother had often sent her down there with fresh bread for his lunch or some such errand. She would always stay longer than she needed to under the great echoing cavern of its roof. Above her the grey pigeons would be flying busily between the steel girders. Down below she would look into the faces of those who waited patiently or impatiently. Some hurried to catch trains, holding on to their hats, their coat-tails flying behind. Others who like her were going nowhere stood or shuffled slowly around. They were there only to pass the time. Some of them were old and lonely. Some of them were young and poor, and they begged or sat around too tired to beg.

She always imagined the travellers were setting out, not 'down the country', but into the depths of China or India or the Wild West like some Jules Verne hero. It was a place above all of adventure, of huge possibilities. The only place, in fact, where she knew for certain that one day she would escape her humdrum existence. Only in Mrs Teehan's drawing room did she feel anything that came near this sense of freedom.

Even now, despite the pain inside her, this rush of tense wonder returned as soon as she stepped into the station. The clamour of noise swept her along. Distant train whistles, steam rising with an ear-splitting hiss, juddering steel beaten, bolts thudding into heavy timber cross-plates, people talking and laughing, barking orders. All these sounds made it impossible for her to think and for that she was grateful.

She was grateful too that they had arrived a little late and when they boarded the train found that they couldn't get seats together.

'We should have kept an eye on the time,' Molly said when they eventually found a single seat for Nora.

'I'm well able to mind myself!' Nora said so sharply that the woman sitting opposite her looked up sternly and Nora cut her with a vicious look.

The woman glared at Molly and went back to her newspaper. After some toing and froing Molly found a seat further along the same carriage. From where she sat Nora could see only the top of her grey head. It was more than she wanted to see of her. She glimpsed the large shoulders of her uncle as he stood between carriages chatting with a group of men. She tried to piece together the little she knew of them. It didn't amount to very much.

They lived in the house where her mother had grown up. Of her grandparents she knew only that they'd died soon after her mother had come to Dublin and married. Molly, who'd married a few years before that moved back into the house with her husband and they took over the running of the shop there. She was now forty years old, six years older than her dead sister. She had no idea how old Peter might be but guessed he must be in his mid-forties.

Nora had always been able to imagine her mother as a young girl but her aunt and uncle seemed so stiff and formal it was hard to believe they had ever known carefree days.

She'd heard mention too of a younger brother to Peter. His name was Jack and, her mother had told her darkly, he had been 'in trouble'. What exactly this 'trouble' had been or whether he was still in it, Nora had no idea. The strange thing was that though she'd never seen his face she thought of it as a more happy one than that of her Uncle Peter.

At last, the train gave a sudden lurch and began to move along by the platform. Now, even the roar of the engine under the station roof was not enough to drown the cry that seemed to rip through her and it took all the strength she could muster to contain it. She thought about leaping from the train before it gathered up speed and imagined herself running back through the crowded station, back to Inchicore and into the street and her own house. As she closed her eyes on a vision of her father sitting drunk by the ash-filled fireplace she knew there was nothing there worth running back to – except the boys, and they would soon be gone.

'I don't care!' she fumed privately.

The woman opposite peered out over her newspaper crossly, exclaiming: 'I beg your pardon!'

'Mind your own business!' Nora shouted and every head in the carriage turned towards her. She sank back, looking at the floor.

However, she wasn't going to be left in peace. The interfering busy-body she'd had the misfortune to sit near was outraged. Turning towards Nora's aunt she called out:

'Is this young strap a child of yours, Missus?'

Molly reddened and at first seemed too intimidated to speak. She spluttered a little foolishly but when her voice came back to her, it was firm and controlled.

'Nora,' she said, 'is my niece and she has enough on her mind without having to put up with the likes of you.'

The woman's jaw dropped and she turned haughtily towards the window muttering to herself. Nora was seized by a mad desire to belt her across the ear. Molly was by her side in an instant:

'Nora, sit over there in my place. I'll sit here.'

'I'm well able to ...'

'... mind yourself! I know that. Just do as I ask.'

Nora stood up and with one last scowl at the busy-body brushed past her aunt. Just then Peter arrived at the scene.

'Is everything all right Molly?'

'We're grand now, aren't we Nora?'

Nora didn't answer. She was glad to get away from the nosy passenger. But admitting this to Molly or thanking her was something she wasn't prepared to do. No matter how much they did for her, no matter what they said she would despise them and this new life she was being forced to lead. Every day, she thought gratefully, would be a day closer to the time when she could escape from them. In the meantime, there was nothing she could do but wait and let life carry her along just as the train did now.

She took no pleasure in seeing for the first time wide-open fields full of cows, sheep and horses; small lazy towns and villages with hardly a soul on their streets; forests of trees, meandering streams, dirt roads and country lanes leading away across the flat plains of Ireland into the huge unknown distance.

The world seemed to her to be nothing more than a big empty space where you could never be sure who was your friend and who your enemy. And you could never be sure if your friends would be there tomorrow or if your enemies would ever go away.

A hand on her shoulder jolted her from her reverie. It was her uncle.

'Five minutes now,' he said, 'and we'll be there.'

Soon, the town rolled into view. She saw a large grey block of a building which stood three storeys high. This surprised her. The picture she had in her mind of the town had always been filled with small, mean cottages and little else.

For a brief moment the carriage darkened under a wide stone bridge. Then in the blaze of new light the train crawled into the station. There was no going on — nor was there any turning back.

Chapter 5

Nora hadn't expected the overwhelming swirl of activity that greeted her as she stepped from the train. A dull, forbidding quiet was what she'd imagined.

What surprised her most was the awesome noise of animals all around her. Cattle roared, donkeys brayed, horses clattered and neighed. Not that any of these things were particularly strange to her in themselves. Indeed, they were to be expected 'down the country'. It was simply that this non-stop chorus never let up as they walked from the platform, into the station yard and on by a long, winding lane into the streets of the town.

Molly noticed her startled interest and laughed.

'Today's a Fair Day, Nora! Don't go thinking it's always like this.'

It was the day when farmers came into town to sell their animals and crops, she explained. Nora was relieved to find this didn't happen every day, if only because the streets wouldn't always be so caked with dung. She'd seen dung before, from the dray horses on the streets of Inchicore. Here, there was more of the stuff than she'd ever stepped through in all her life! And the smell of it was impossible to escape. She lifted the hem of her skirt gingerly to avoid being splashed with it.

In spite of the fact that he was already carrying two bags, Peter offered to carry hers too. She gave him a withering look and held her bag tightly to herself. A great change had come over Molly and Peter once they left the train. Gone was the straight-backed formality of the previous days. Now they were calm and contented.

'This is Friary Street,' Molly announced as they reached the end of the lane from the station. Up ahead there seemed to Nora to be more animals than people. Half-way down this street Peter, who walked a few paces in front, waved to a tall black-haired man working in a garage.

'Good day, Mick!'

'Mr Delaney! How are ye all?' the man called in a deep sing-song accent.

'Not too bad, considering, Mick,' Peter called.

'Sorry for your troubles, Molly,' the man said.

'Thanks, Mick. I know you are,' she answered with a weak smile.

'Will you have a look at the generator for me this evening?' Peter asked.

The man raised his thumb in assent and Peter moved on. There was a spring in his step Nora hadn't noticed before and all along the street people called to him while others spoke quietly to Molly, shaking their heads sympathetically.

'This is her young one,' she would say. 'Nora. A grand girl.' And they would look with understanding in their eyes and whisper:

'Ah, God help us!'

Nora might have been more irritated if it hadn't been for her curiosity at the strange questions directed at Peter from all sides.

'Did you get any new ones, Mr Delaney?' one man asked.

'I believe you're going ahead on Friday night. Aren't you great all the same and all the troubles you have!' an almost toothless old woman cried.

'We all have troubles these days,' he told her. 'If we can forget for a while mightn't it ease them?'

'Well, Peter,' another man asked, good-humouredly, 'Have you something for Friday night?'

To all these questions Peter had the same answer. He would hold up the small leather case he carried, tapping it, and joke mysteriously, 'Can't let the cat out of the bag yet!'

Soon they were in the centre of town. As soon as Molly mentioned that this wide quadrangle was called the Square, Nora remembered her mother talking about the place. This was where she'd spent her early days working in a solicitor's office. She always sounded relieved to have escaped the musty rooms and the cantankerous old man with his bush of rust-grey hair who lorded over her.

Stretching away ahead of them was a higgledy-piggledy gathering of carts of all shapes and sizes right down the centre of the Square. Here were displayed potatoes, carrots, churns of milk, straw bedding, horse hair, tin cans, turf and much more that was unrecognisable to Nora. Horses and donkeys were tethered in various places resting from their exertions in carting all of this into town.

On the footpath, the shops showed off their wares too. Tea-chests and timber barrels full of heaven knows what; heavy boots and horse tackle hanging from awnings; and in the windows fine clothes and hats and shoes.

All around her, farmers and townspeople made deals and

haggled and cursed loudly. Barefoot children chased each other through the crowd and others with straw boaters and shiny boots stepped carefully between the puddles that were everywhere. Whether rich or poor the children, she thought, eyed her with the same suspicion. She glared back at them as if warning them off.

Peter was busy deflecting another question when he almost collided with a man in army uniform who just then stepped out from a shop. Nora was so taken aback that her hand went instinctively towards her aunt's. Just as suddenly she withdrew it.

The two men stood apart and the officer slipped off the glove from his right hand. His cold expression softened. He thrust his hand towards Peter and said with a deep sigh, 'Sorry for your troubles, Peter.'

'Thanks, Gerry.'

'And yourself, Molly,' he went on, 'I couldn't credit it when they told me about poor Annie.'

Once again, Nora was introduced and told to say hello to Colonel O'Brien. He was about Peter's age and his hair too was thin. Not as tall as Peter, he was heavier around the stomach and his cheeks were a high reddish-purple colour. She fully expected him to mutter the usual, 'God help us'.

'Your mother'll never be gone while you're around,' he told her instead and to Molly he added, 'She's the image of her, isn't she?'

They talked sadly for a few minutes about Michael Collins, and how he would be missed in the long years ahead. Soon, however, Nora sensed a hesitancy coming over her uncle and the officer. It was the Colonel at last, who spoke decisively:

'We had a bit of a problem last night, Peter.'

Peter grew apprehensive and shifted uneasily from one foot to the other.

'Surely not in town with all the men you have!' Peter exclaimed.

'Right here in the Square. They robbed the Munster and Leinster Bank.'

Peter was pale now. The Colonel went on speaking.

'I was in Dublin myself and this new fellow they sent me, Captain Doyle, he took every last man out of town. He got word of an ambush out in Borris. Left the damn place wide open for them!'

'And there was no ambush, I suppose,' Peter said wearily.

'Not at all,' Colonel O'Brien muttered.

Molly was trying to draw Nora's attention to the shop window behind them and away from what was being said. Nora looked reluctantly at the dress her aunt was pointing to. She kept an ear to the conversation continuing close by.

'Was the lad in on it, do you think?' Peter asked mysteriously.

'I hope not, Peter,' the Colonel told him, 'All we know is one of them was wearing glasses. We found a small piece of spectacle lens near the vault so we checked with the clerks and it wasn't any of theirs.'

'At least the lad doesn't wear glasses,' Peter smiled ruefully, 'but he's blind anyway getting caught up with that crowd.'

'Not half as blind as this Doyle fellow,' Colonel O'Brien added.

All this mysterious talk was beginning to infuriate Nora. When her aunt asked if she'd like to go into the shop it was less from rudeness than curiosity that she shook her head vehemently. Ignoring Molly she wondered who 'the lad' might be and who was this buffoon called Captain Doyle?

'Peter,' the Colonel said with a hint of desperation in his voice, 'I know you're an honest man. We soldiered together when the real fight was on with the Black 'n' Tans. But do you have no idea where the lad might be? We've had no bother in town up to this and I don't want this class of thing going on. I don't believe he does either. Whatever else he might be, he's not a common thief.'

'I haven't seen him since this thing started up and I don't want to see him 'til it's over,' Peter said firmly. 'Maybe not even then!'

'If I could only talk to him, I know we could work something out. But for God's sake, Peter, watch out for this Doyle fellow. He's bad news and dead set on taking in the lad. He's put in a few requests already to raid your house and he's hardly here a month.'

'I've nothing to hide, Gerry.'

'I know that but I don't trust this fellow to obey my orders. He might be a fool but he's a dangerous one.'

'Thanks for the warning,' Peter said, 'I appreciate it.'

'Did we ever think it would come to this?' the Colonel sighed. 'The best of friends at one another's throats!'

Nora turned and saw they were shaking hands again. Colonel O'Brien lifted his hat to Molly and Nora and went away busily pulling on his glove. Close behind, two young soldiers with rifles broke into a trot to keep up with him.

Peter walked a little less lightly now, his heavy step more like what you might expect from the big man he was. Now he answered the calls of the townspeople with a shrug of the shoulders. He switched his bag from one hand to the other as if the weight had suddenly become too much for him to bear.

They crossed a wide stone bridge over a quietly flowing river. Molly informed Nora they were in Church Street. Here there was a curious mixture of rather grand buildings and tiny thatched cottages that somehow didn't belong together. The largest building rose four storeys from the footpath and had row upon row of windows looking out on to the street.

'That's where your mother went to school,' her aunt said.

Her mother had never spoken of her schooldays. Nora guessed she must have been very unhappy there and looking at this huge hulk of a place she could well imagine why. It reminded her at once of Kilmainham Jail, near her home in Inchicore.

'And you'll follow her footsteps, won't you, Nora?' Molly added.

Nora pretended not to hear. They passed by the church and on beyond some more cottages where women in the doorways greeted her aunt and uncle. As soon as they'd gone by, the women came together to wonder aloud about the girl walking forlornly between Mr and Mrs Delaney.

At the end of Church Street the road divided in two. They followed the street that veered to the right. This was Stannix Lane, Molly announced proudly, where Nora's new home was to be.

The first building on their left was a public house. From inside its doors came a raucous din of rough conversation and laughter and clinking glasses. Outside on the roadway stood several ponies and traps and a few asses and carts.

When they had come within a few yards of the place, the noise suddenly became louder and then was muffled again. The door had opened and there appeared on the pavement before them a most extraordinary sight. At least for Nora it was extraordinary. Molly and Peter hardly blinked an eyelid.

The man who stepped rather shakily out of the pub was unlike any of the other people she'd so far seen in the town. For one thing he wasn't wearing the usual black or dark brown suit that other men wore. Instead, he was dressed in a bright, if shabby, cream-coloured suit. Around his neck was a garish yellow dicky bow. A pair of tight black leather gloves contrasted strangely with his colourful outfit.

'Blind drunk again,' Peter whispered to Molly.

'The poor wretch!' she said and they both looked at him with real concern.

The man made a very obvious attempt to screw his eyes into focus. Nora was surprised to notice that he seemed quite young. In fact, his face was almost handsome, but haunted too – a face that was ill-shaven, even unclean, and that yet was difficult to take your eyes from. It was as if, by staring long enough at it, you would discover what terrible tragedy had reduced him to this state.

'Mr Smithson,' Peter addressed him: 'Won't you come up and have the tea with us?'

The man still seemed doubtful as to who these three people standing before him were. He reeled back into the pub to a thunderous roar of whistles and jeers.

'Poor Alec,' Molly sighed. 'He's killing himself.'

Memories of Nora's father flooded back to her now and she cowered away from the door. Molly put an arm around her reassuringly.

'He wouldn't hurt a fly, Nora,' she said and added as if in explanation. 'He's our piano-man.'

Nora wriggled free. She couldn't stand being touched by this wrecker of her family. The emptiness in her heart left by her absent mother, her uncaring father and her innocent brothers returned. She switched her thoughts to the mysteries thrown up as they walked through town. What was in Peter's bag? What was to happen on Friday night? What was a piano-man and what on earth did her aunt and uncle want one for? Finally, who was 'the lad' and who were the 'crowd', as Peter had put it, he was mixed up with? Could it possibly be Peter's brother, Jack, the one who'd been in trouble before?

They stopped at a narrow three-storey house. Over the

door, a small sign bore her mother's family name, 'Hickeys'. Peter unlocked the door and Nora entered on a tide of fear, resentment and doubt.

Chapter 6

'We'd better throw some light on the subject!' Peter declared, as they plunged into the half-dark of the shop. He pulled back the curtains on the front window and Nora found herself standing on the rough, clean floorboards her mother had crossed over and back all the years of her childhood.

Close by, a timber counter spanned the width of the room. Behind it were shelves of groceries, bags of meal and flour. From the ceiling hung sides of bacon on iron hooks and on a special rack outside the counter stood a pile of newspapers.

'This is the shop,' Molly said as if she couldn't think what else to say.

Nora resisted the temptation to snigger. Peter placed his mysterious bag on the counter near the window and went down the far end to open the hatch allowing Nora and Molly through.

The door behind the counter led into a narrow hallway. Molly went about showing the rooms to Nora, putting up patiently with the girl's glum indifference.

First along the hallway was a small room Molly called the store. Next, came the parlour, a carefully decorated and spotless place with silver candlesticks and finely waxed and polished furniture. It was, Molly laughed, the biggest room in the house and the one least used. Beyond this were the kitchen and scullery — not very different in size or content to the one Nora had spent so much time in until now.

Up a steep and poorly-lit stairs were two bedrooms, one on each side of the landing. One looked out on to the street and the other, on to the backs of buildings on the street behind. From this landing a last set of steps led to the one room on the top floor.

Nora's feet had only touched the timbers of that first step when the raw ice of her spirit began to melt. Before she could even begin to think why, she knew the room above was no ordinary room. She reached for the handle of the door. It opened as easily to her touch as if someone in there had been waiting for her to come.

'This was Mam's room,' she said with absolute certainty, and her aunt nodded.

Light streamed in from the windows at both ends of the room. There was a brass bed with a small table alongside. On a neat lace cloth at the centre stood an elegant oil lamp. Under the window and to her left was a washstand with a cream and blue flower-patterned jug and basin. In the corner to her right was a mirrored wardrobe, so large that Nora clutched her meagre bundle of clothes to herself shyly.

She moved across to the window which towered above the street. Down below people passed by unaware that she was watching them. Alongside this window was a dresser with four large drawers underneath and a pair of mirrored doors on top. Oblivious to her aunt's presence she turned the tiny key and opened it.

There were four shelves filled to overflowing with books of all shapes and sizes.

'I think you'll like this room,' Molly said.

'Yes, I will,' Nora answered without a trace of malice.

'Grand,' Molly sighed with great relief, 'I'll leave you to sort yourself out while I get the tea.'

She went away hopeful that her niece might, after all, settle down with them.

Soon, Nora could hear pots and pans rattling way below and the smell of cooking wasn't long in reaching the top of the house. She lay back on the bed and closed her eyes sure that if she waited long enough her mother's girlhood spirit would come close. She wanted to raise her arms and reach out to her but they were tied down by some invisible burden. Her fingers too were stiff like in the days of her first piano lessons. She no longer drifted easily as a leaf on the breeze. Instead she felt like a rock on the ground, and her heart was a great weight within her.

'Nora!'

She jumped from the bed, moving her hands and arms about to prove to herself that she hadn't turned to stone.

'Nora!' Molly called, 'the tea's ready.'

Peter was already sitting at the table when she reached the kitchen. Before him were two piles of paper slips which he examined carefully as he wrote figures into a ledger. Without looking up from his work he said, 'You must be wall-falling with the hunger!'

'Not really,' Nora lied but at that moment her stomach gave a tell-tale rumble.

'By cripes, Molly! Was that thunder or what?'

Nora was livid. It was bad enough to have made a show of herself but to be made fun of too was adding insult to injury.

'Don't laugh at me!' she said sharply.

Peter put his pen down, gathered the slips of paper together and closed the ledger. He pointed at the chair next to
his.

'This is your seat, Nora,' he said. 'Sit down, please.'

The request was so unexpectedly polite that she found
herself sitting and eating heartily without another word of
protest. Half-way through the meal Peter spoke up and it was
as if he was addressing a meeting rather than two people at
a kitchen table. He fixed his gaze on a spot above the big
cooker.

'These are difficult times we're living in. If we can't have
a bit of a laugh we might as well throw in the towel altogether.'

'True for you,' Molly agreed.

'Are you sure about Friday night, Molly?' he asked
gravely. 'After everything that's happened. Tell me if you
think I'm wrong to go ahead with it.'

'People depend on us for a bit of a lift,' she said. 'We can't
let our own woes get in the way of that.'

Nora had no idea what they were talking about but she felt
that somehow they were making little of her mother's passing. She might have said so had her attention not been dis-
tracted as she moved her feet uneasily under the table. At first
she was sure she had touched accidentally off Peter's foot.
However, when she peered down below she saw that between her foot and the leg of the table stood her uncle's
mystery bag. It was ever so slightly open.

She reckoned that if she could manage to squeeze the
lower part of the bag against the leg of the table, the top would
open out so that she could see inside. She began to do just this
while at the same time eating vigorously. Getting the food
from plate to mouth was quite difficult with her eyes focused

on the slowly unfolding mystery below. Twice, in fact, the fork aimed at her mouth ended up pressing its load against her cheek. Luckily her aunt and uncle were too engrossed in conversation or, perhaps, too polite to notice.

With great effort, she forced a gap of at least two inches at the top of the bag. She cut a sausage awkwardly and raised it slowly as she traced the outline of a large, flat metal box with a label on its side.

She squinted hard but the words on the label remained dizzily elusive. In the meantime, she had completely forgotten about the half-sausage suspended somewhat shakily from her fork between the table and her right ear. In horror, she saw it drop into view and down into the bag. She looked up, dumbstruck.

'Are you all right?' Molly asked.

'What is it?' Peter chipped in.

'My sausage,' Nora answered, feeling like a complete idiot, 'fell!'

'Never mind, it's only a sausage.' Peter grinned.

'It ... it fell into your bag.' Nora explained.

'My bag?' Peter exclaimed, his eyebrows arched high, and banged the table with his first.

Nora almost fell of her chair with shock. She trembled fearfully until she realised her uncle wasn't shaking with rage but with laughter. He let out a loud whoop and wiped the tears from his eyes.

'Isn't that a good one!' he roared.

Molly began to chuckle too and even Nora allowed a smile of relief to break through her scowl. Peter lifted the bag on to the table and after rummaging around for a moment or two produced the sausage, like a rabbit out of a hat. This set him into hysterics again and several moments passed before he emptied out the rest of the contents. There were envelopes and sheets of paper, a fountain pen and finally the metal box. It was bigger than a dinner plate and had a faded, silvery look. She swallowed her pride and asked him directly,

'What's in the box?'

No sooner had she spoken than she was angry with herself for giving in so easily to her curiosity. It was almost like a betrayal to show interest in anything so soon after her mother's death. But she did want to know what the box contained.

'This, my dear,' Peter announced grandly, 'is a film!'

Nora stared at him blankly.

'And what, you may well ask, is a grocer and news-vendor doing with a moving picture on his premises?' he continued in exaggerated tones.

He stood up and motioned to her.

'Follow me, young woman!'

'God, Peter, it's nearly dark out there,' Molly said, 'And she'll freeze!'

'Not at all,' he laughed, lighting up an oil lamp, 'We'll be back in five minutes.'

He lifted the latch on the back door and held it open for her. Nora was stuck to her chair not because she was afraid to go out into the dark but because she was fighting against her foolish inquisitiveness.

'Are you coming or what?' he called and she stood up like a puppet being moved about by some force outside herself.

The evening light was fading fast but it was just about bright enough for her to see the small cobbled yard with two outhouses at the end. At the back wall was a timber door which led out on to a narrow and long-neglected lane overgrown with wild grass and weeds. A short trail of flattened grass led from the door they'd passed through to another door on the wall opposite.

Again there was a cobbled yard but this one was more spacious. Here also were more sheds and outhouses and the building beyond was, perhaps, three or four times wider than her aunt and uncle's house. Peter swung back the door of one of the outhouses and, holding up the lamp, called her over.

'Here's our generator,' he whispered as if were top secret, 'Only for Mick at the garage above there'd never be a show.'

Nora peered inside but the black snake-like coil of heavy wire and the complicated machine meant nothing to her.

'What's it for?' she asked.

'The Lord said, "Let there be light",' he declaimed, 'and there was this!'

She was still puzzled and it showed.

'The light, you see! That projects the pictures up on the screen.'

She nodded her head.

'But sure, what am I telling a city girl like yourself for. I bet you've seen any amount of pictures up there.'

Only once had she ever been to see a film. Her mother had taken her to see the story of Joan of Arc in a theatre up in Phibsboro. It had been a reward for another spectacular success with Mrs Teehan. She loved the story and never forgot what her mother had said when they came out.

'There you are, Nora. A woman can do as much as any man and be just as brave and, by God, in this world she has to be!'

In the meantime, Peter had unlocked yet another door and stepped inside the large building. Nora moved closer as he plunged into the pitch darkness ahead. She almost had to run to keep up with him as he went through the vast shadowy hall that was filled with ranks of chairs and long benches.

'This,' he told her, 'is the Parnell Hall.'

Nora looked behind her and saw, in the weak light from the lantern, a stage closed off by heavy velvet curtains of scarlet red with gold braid along its edges.

'Or should I say,' Peter went on, 'it's the Parnell Hall during the week.'

He walked across, shoes banging out huge echoes, to where an old stained sheet lay, covering a long length of board. The board stood about the height of a chairback and Nora counted eight chairs along its length. Peter set the oil lamp on the floor.

The long panel was painted a deep evening-sky blue, a sky studded with stars distant and near, of all colours. Forming a neat arch in the centre and painted in gold was the word *'Stella'*. Below, enclosed by the arch of glittering letters, a message screamed out, *'Come see the Stars!'*

'It's the "Stella"!' Peter beamed. ' "Come see the stars," do you see. Because *"Stella"* is the Latin word for star!'

'Oh!' Nora replied.

'Eight weeks we're on the go now and never missed a week,' he said proudly. 'To be honest, I thought we might give it a rest this Friday coming after ... the funeral and all ... but Molly insisted. I hope you don't mind, Nora.'

She shrugged her shoulders dismissively. It made no difference what they did, she would have no part in it in any case. As far as she was concerned she was still in mourning even if they thought entertaining strangers was more important.

Peter pointed out the threepenny seats up the front, the 'sixpenny' in the main body of the Hall and the 'shilling' seats barely visible in the small balcony at the far end.

'Only twenty-four of them,' he told her. 'So, they'll be here an hour before the show to get them.'

He crossed by the front of the stage and stepped in behind a makeshift curtain. It reached to his shoulders so that he could look out over it and call her in.

'Have a look at this!'

Nora was becoming annoyed at his boundless enthusiasm. She was disappointed too that what should have been a marvellous discovery, a cinema in her back garden, held no excitement for her beyond those first moments of surprise.

Peter drew back the curtain and there, in all its glory, a deep-brown, highly veneered piano with two freshly polished brass candelabras on its gleaming front. Below, however, a set of stained and chipped ivories hinted at the instrument's true age. This was obviously Mr Smithson, the piano-man's, perch.

'What about a blast of a tune?' Peter exclaimed. 'Mrs Teehan told us you were a dinger at it!'

'No, I'm not,' Nora muttered.

'Ah, go on!' he insisted.

'I don't want to!' she answered and shot him a vicious glare.

She was going to add, 'Ever again!' but he raised his hands as if to protect himself and grinned.

'God protect us from fiery women!'

'And stupid men!'

Peter was taken aback but kept up his smiling determination to stay in good humour no matter what. He gritted his teeth and walked to the other end of the hall and on up to the balcony. Nora followed him reluctantly.

There, he showed where he'd neatly chipped out the blocks from the wall for the projector to shine through. He brought her into the tiny space behind the balcony where the projector stood and explained, in great detail, how the reel was clamped on and how it was moved by a series of cogs and wheels and how the lens was operated to focus the images on the screen and all the problems there were and how they might be solved.

She was beginning to feel cold and ungrateful and wanted to burst the bubble of his high spirits. She decided to test her suspicion of who 'the lad' might be. If it really was his brother, that would certainly bring him back to painful reality.

'Who is "the lad"?' she asked as he paused momentarily for breath in his hurried talk.

He exhaled slowly.

'The lad?'

'You and that Colonel fellow talked about the lad like it was someone you know very well.'

Peter was hurt, she could see that. She almost smiled.

'Who is he?' she snapped.

'My brother, Jack,' he said finally. 'We always called him "the lad".'

'And you think,' she said wide-eyed, 'he might have robbed the bank?'

'I don't know. I don't know what to think any more. He's with the Irregulars.'

Nora began to move back towards the door but he continued talking. Her mind was filled with her father's stories of the cruelty and thuggery of the Irregulars. As if reading her mind, he said, 'I've nothing to do with that crowd. I couldn't fight against my own people. It's madness. I pleaded with him not to go but he wouldn't listen.'

She reached the door by now and turned to run to the stairs.

'I swear to you, Nora, you'll be safe here. The town is too well guarded.'

What kind of place and among what kind of dangerous people had she been plunged, she wondered in growing horror?

'Nora!' he called after her, 'You'll lose your way in the dark.'

But it was already too late. The stairs had loomed up too quickly on her and she was tumbling away with his scream ringing in her ears. The silence after her fall was so complete that Peter froze to the spot at the head of the stairs and stared helplessly at her crumpled, motionless figure.

Chapter 7

Nora woke in her room. Her body ached and only slowly did she realise where the sharpest pains were lodged. She had fallen on her right side and here her elbow and ankle throbbed fiercely. The effort of opening her eyes was, for the moment, too much to make and she lay quite still, listening.

Because her head was spinning so much she couldn't at first make sense of the voices which filled the room. She had the impression that a crowd of people were standing around her staring curiously. Soon, however, she recognised the tones of her aunt and uncle interrupted from time to time by those of a stranger.

'I'm sure,' the stranger said, 'there's a bone broken in the elbow or maybe just cracked. Either way she won't be using it for a while.'

'Oh, God! Peter, what are we going to do?' Molly cried.

'It was all my fault,' he said miserably.

'If she has trouble with playing the piano,' Molly said, 'we could never forgive ourselves.'

The thought hadn't occurred to Nora until Molly blurted it out. Now that she had a real reason to stop playing she wasn't sure quite how she felt about it. Then the stranger spoke up.

'She'll get back to it if she wants to and no amount of discomfort will stop her.'

In the silence that followed Nora gradually began to notice the tightness of what must, she guessed, be a bandage on her elbow. She thought about opening her eyes but in the end decided she wanted to avoid seeing her aunt and uncle or speaking to them — especially her uncle who had frightened her with his talk of the Irregulars. She didn't feel she could ever trust him now.

After a little while Molly spoke to the stranger again.

'You should come downstairs and eat something.'

'I'd prefer to wait until she comes out of it,' the man said. 'You can tell a lot from that, you know. How they react when they wake.'

'Maybe,' Molly said, 'we should get in touch with her father. What do you think, Peter?'

Nora sat up and fixed Molly with an angry glare.

'Don't bother telling *him*!' she hissed. 'He couldn't wait to get rid of me anyway!'

She flopped back on to the pillow. Her brain pounded into her forehead.

'Try not to move around, Nora,' the stranger said and she turned to look at him.

It was Mr Smithson, the cream-suited piano-man. She stared at him in revulsion.

'What's he doing here? He's a drunk!'

'Nora!' Molly said, shocked at her directness. 'He's sober as a judge and he's after fixing you up grand!'

'It's all right,' Mr Smithson said, 'just move your leg up

and down and we'll see is there any more damage done.'

'I won't,' Nora cried and then feeling another twinge of pain in her ankle, muttered, 'I can't.'

Eventually he located the problem and began to bandage up the foot. He showed no signs of unsteadiness but never once, as he worked, did he remove the black gloves she had noticed earlier. When he saw how she was puzzled by this he told her with a wistful smile,

'Old war wounds. Not a pleasant sight, you know!'

'Are you a doctor?' she asked him suspiciously.

'Not exactly,' he said, 'but I was a medical student for a few years.'

'He's as good, if not better, than any doctor in this town,' Molly interjected.

'Thank you, Mrs Delaney,' he smiled not sounding very convinced.

'Did you fight the Black 'n' Tans too?' Nora asked.

'Nora!' Molly cried.

'No, I'm afraid I fought alongside the old enemy in the Great War over in France.'

It didn't surprise her that he'd been in the British Army. In fact, it seemed to fit in perfectly with this sense of his being different. What did surprise her was that he and her uncle, who had fought against the British, were apparently such good friends. She'd often heard her father describe fights in the bars he frequented, between Republicans and ex-British soldiers — all of them nonetheless Irish men.

'How would you fancy a couple of weeks in bed?' Mr Smithson said, changing the subject.

'I'll be fine in the morning.'

'Indeed you won't,' he told her. 'You've had a bad fall and a right good knock on the head.'

'Better to be safe than sorry,' Peter added, trying to be cheerful.

'I'll be keeping a check on you for a day or two, just in case,' said the man in the cream suit as he got up to go.

'Say thanks to Mr Smithson!' Molly insisted.

'Thanks,' Nora offered half-heartedly and they left her.

Mr Smithson's voice carried through from the landing outside.

'Make sure to call me now if there's any change in her. And don't worry, I won't be drinking. Not until we see this through!'

The prospect of lying alone in her room for hours and days on end seemed exactly what Nora wanted. There would be little or no contact with her aunt and uncle, no work, no school and no piano. It couldn't have worked out better really, except for the relentless aching in her limbs. Even this seemed worthwhile as she lay in the comfortable surroundings of her mother's girlhood.

During the next few days she dozed almost all of the time. When she woke it was to a strange world somewhere between dream and nightmare. If she expected darkness it would certainly be broad daylight. If she expected morning she found herself plunged into night. When the pain kept her suspended between sleep and waking she imagined her mother here in this room, dreaming innocently of some grand future. The thought of how those dreams had been shattered hurt Nora more than the pain in her body. She vowed never to be fooled by the childish hope that led you to expect great wonders in your life and, in the end, left you disappointed.

Late in the evening of her third day in bed she stirred fitfully again into wakefulness. The oil lamp hadn't yet been lit but there was enough light from the street to catch a glimpse of a figure sitting on the window-sill. In a split second the room was suddenly pitch-black again. In her drowsy state, Nora was convinced she'd gone blind. She began to shake uncontrollably.

'It's only the Glimmer Man,' a voice whispered, 'knocking off the street lamps.'

In the bright, momentary flare of a struck match she saw Mr Smithson raising the glass from the oil lamp.

'There you go,' he said cheerfully.

'Ye flippin' eejit,' she burst out. 'You frightened the life out of me!'

'Sorry.'

'What are you doing in my room, anyway?' she snarled, pulling the sheets up around her.

'Peter and Molly had to go out for a while,' he explained, a faint trace of a smile turning the corner of his lips. 'You're a tough lady!'

'You're no prize gentleman yourself!'

'True for you,' he laughed and they both fell silent and avoided looking in each other's direction.

Finally, Mr Smithson spoke up again.

'I hear you're a bit of a wizard on the piano, is that right?'

'You shouldn't believe everything you hear!'

'And I don't. But Peter told me ...'

Nora cut him off with a steely glance.

'I don't want to talk about it and I don't want to see another piano. Ever!'

'That's foolish talk,' he began but again she interrupted him.

'It's the truth.'

'I told myself the same thing once,' he said, holding up his gloved hands. 'Told myself I'd never play again but I found a way to and I'd be even worse off than I am now, if I hadn't.'

Nora turned away and sulked into her pillow.

'Get out of here,' she cried. 'You're making my headache worse.'

'Whatever you say,' he declared. 'Just try not to lift your head and, for God's sake, don't be getting excited, I'm just an old fool, talking nonsense.'

'Yes, you are!'

'I'll be outside on the landing if you want me, Nora,' he called from the doorway.

'I won't be wanting you. And don't dare call me Nora.'

'Well, you can call me Alec, if you like,' he joked.

'I know what I'd like to call you all right!'

'Sorry, sorry,' he said, closing out the door.

She decided to tell her aunt and uncle she didn't want him around her. If necessary she would even pretend she'd seen him drinking from a whiskey bottle there. It was a cruel notion, she knew, but in her foul mood it seemed quite reasonable.

The next morning found her much brighter and the sun blazing in by the window felt good. Her elbow still throbbed and her foot was stiff and heavy. Nevertheless, when her aunt came in with her breakfast on a tray she told her, without having to be coaxed, that she felt much better.

'We'll have you up and about in no time,' Molly said happily.

Nora ate ravenously as Molly went about freshening up the room. The breeze from the open window brought with it a new sense of vitality and more surprisingly a feeling of quiet satisfaction. She wondered if last night's argument with Mr Smithson hadn't been a new beginning of sorts. Certainly she felt less miserably unhappy. She was even inclined to believe what her uncle had said about this town being a safe place. The fall, she acknowledged privately, had been mainly her own fault. Even the conversation that had come before it had been started by her.

'Could I sit by the window?' she asked Molly.

'I suppose so,' her aunt said uncertainly. 'But not for long.'

Nora threw back the sheets with her good arm. Molly escorted her carefully, taking the weight of Nora's right side, and after a bit of a struggle got her to the window. The sun was warm on her face and she thanked her aunt.

'There's no need to thank me at all. Seeing you like this is thanks enough.'

Molly fussed around her for a while, taking out a shawl and draping it over her shoulders and wrapping a blanket around her legs. As she moved about her expression slowly changed from content to worry. Nora grew apprehensive watching this unexpected turnabout.

'You're uncle's in a bad way over what happened,' she said finally. 'Maybe I shouldn't ask, but would you say something to him? He's afraid even to come up and look in on you.'

'I wouldn't know what to say,' Nora muttered and, in her own mind added, 'Even if I really wanted to.'

'Well, what if I just tell him you don't bear any grudge against him? Would that be all right?'

Nora shrugged her shoulders. She felt she was being forced, in the nicest possible way of course, into making a peace she didn't yet feel ready for. At the same time, she realised that for the time being she was stuck in this place and, as her mother used to tell her, you have to make the best of things. Finally, she nodded her agreement. Molly couldn't contain her delight and went downstairs straight off to reassure Peter.

Outside the street was quiet with just the occasional passer-by moving slowly along. Watching their unhurried progress was a welcome relief from the hectic events of the past few days.

The house too was quiet at first but as the morning passed she noticed a flurry of activity below. There was much toing and froing out in the back yard and every so often she heard the ringing sound of metal banging on metal. When Peter came upstairs to see her the cause of all this bustle was explained.

'How are you today, girl?' he asked. 'I hear you're on the mend!'

'I'm fine, thanks.'

He came and stood near her at the window.

'Isn't it a powerful day out there,' he said, lost in thought. 'Wouldn't you think people would be happy with that and not be fighting over a scrap of paper?'

Nora moved uncomfortably, unsure of what to say.

'There I go again,' he sighed. 'Upsetting you with my troubles. I'm sorry about the other night.'

This was altogether new for Nora, being apologised to. Her father could never bring himself to do such a thing and he often had every reason to with Nora and with her mother.

'I get so worried about Jack,' he continued. 'And even if he did rob the bank, and I don't believe he did, he's still my brother. You can understand that, can't you?'

She tried to speak but could only manage a low mutter.

'Can we forget about all that now and make a new start?' he asked and reached out his hand. 'Friends?'

She offered him her good hand.

'A pity you can't come to the pictures tonight,' he smiled. 'Maybe next week, what!'

So that was it. Friday night had come and all the commotion was in preparation for the transformation of the Parnell Hall into the Stella Cinema. She was a little disappointed but glad too. The truth was she didn't yet feel ready to re-enter the world that still held so many uncertainties for her.

Later in the evening after Molly had brought her tea and left the house to join Peter at the hall, silence descended once again. As the time dragged on she found she couldn't sleep. In the end, she struggled out of bed and, supporting herself against the wall, made her way to the back window.

She moved the oil lamp on to the window-sill and sat down beside it. A sharp pain darted through her elbow as she unlatched the window and opened it a bare inch or so.

The cool night air chilled her and she pulled the shawl close. She listened to the sounds from the hall opposite. The generator hummed gently as a loud cheer filled the night. A roll on the piano followed and then a huge chorus of gasping breaths.

Even from this distance she knew that Alec Smithson, for all his foolishness, could really play very well. There was a hush out there now filled only with a soft, haunting melody. She swayed to the rhythm and let it carry her away as if to some golden time. She wondered whether she might have been able to forgive her father his uncaring cruelty and his drinking if he could have played like this.

Suddenly she had a strange feeling that someone was watching her. Jerking her head back she grimaced at the stabbing pain in her elbow. There was no-one in the room; of that she was certain. She listened closely but the house was deathly quiet. She peered down into the yard below.

There, in the faint light from the hall, she saw a man leaning back against an outhouse door. He stared upwards in her direction as if he'd seen a ghost.

Chapter 8

Nora could not have known what a strange figure she presented to the man in the yard below. Her face, lit from beneath by the oil lamp, gave an impression of other-worldliness. All the more so when fear transfixed it.

The man began to stir himself from his frozen terror and appeared to take a hesitant step forward. Nora gasped and retreated a little from the window. She heard him scurry across the yard but before she could catch a glimpse of his face he had disappeared. She let out the breath she had been holding, sure that the danger had passed.

Then a heavy footstep hit the boards of the first step on the stairs below. Footstep followed footstep as Nora called:

'Uncle Peter, is that you?' and then, 'Is that you, Molly?'

There was no reply and whoever the stranger was he had now reached the first landing. Nora's throat was dry.

The intruder began to mount the last flight of steps. Nora moved along by the wall, keeping her injured foot off the ground, but lost her balance just as she reached the door. It slammed shut as she stumbled against it. She slid down and pressed with all her strength on its frail timbers.

It could only be a matter of seconds now. The heavy tread came so close that she could hear his uneven breath. Somehow she was reminded of her mother's gasping for breath in those last days. It was the unmistakable sound of sickness.

The handle of the door turned and she whispered desperately:

'Please leave me alone!'

The door opened an inch in spite of her efforts to hold it closed. Then there was a moment of hesitancy, a moment charged with terror and foreboding. Nora knew he was trying to decide what to do next and she prayed he would have pity on her. Her body ached as if to remind her how helpless she would be if he decided to push the door again.

'Please leave me alone!' she called out.

In an instant the pressure was released. On the landing the footsteps retreated, paused again and began to run down the stairs. Nora crawled across to the window determined to catch sight of the man as he emerged into the yard. She got there just in time to see him open an outhouse door and gather up some things hurriedly. Then, with perfect timing, the pictures ended in the hall with a big cheer and the lights went up, shining brightly into the dim space below.

The man turned suddenly on hearing the noise from the hall and his face was caught in the streaming light. Nora stared fixedly. There was no recognition at first. He swung round again and made off down the overgrown lane. As he took one fleeting glance backwards Nora was certain for a moment that it was Peter. It didn't seem to make sense until the realisation burst upon her that it had to be his brother, Jack, the Irregular. The similarity was unmistakable.

Out in the yard she heard her aunt calling to someone.

'Wasn't it a grand show!'

'Bring tears to your eyes, it would,' a woman answered.

It made Nora feel secure again to hear this normal chit-chat. She hauled herself back over to the bed and lay down, listening to the noises from the dark street.

Children laughed and shouted and there was the loud clatter of many feet clumping and skittering away into the night. Her uncle's voice reached her too above all the din.

'Great little machine, that generator,' he was saying proudly.

'It is indeed,' Mick from the garage replied. 'You got a right bargain there.'

Nora had a real problem on her hands now. It should have been easy for her simply to go ahead and tell Peter that his brother had been hiding in the outhouse. There was no good reason for her to want to protect him after he had so terrorised her. And yet, he had left her alone when she'd pleaded and the face she had briefly seen had given no impression of evil. If anything that face had seemed to demand her sympathy. They were both, she felt, outcasts in their different ways.

She couldn't believe she was thinking like this and tried again to convince herself that Jack was nothing more than a common criminal. Everything she had ever heard about the Irregulars pointed to this. Her mother had taught her to despise dishonesty and yet Nora had seen her hide the truth from her father to avoid his anger. Her sense of responsibility was overwhelmed with nagging doubts. Shouldn't she reassure Peter who was so worried at not knowing where his brother was?

If she did tell him couldn't Peter arrange for Jack to meet Colonel O'Brien and sit down to talk about peace?

Then again mightn't Colonel O'Brien just lay a trap for Jack? How could she be sure the Colonel wanted only to talk?

Would Peter himself betray Jack, if only to get him away from the fighting?

And perhaps Peter knew all along where Jack was? Perhaps he was hiding him and merely putting on a show of concern?

When Molly came quietly to the door thinking she might be asleep, Nora still hadn't made up her mind as to what she should do.

'Did you sleep at all?' Molly wondered as she looked in around the door and saw Nora wide awake.

'I did,' Nora lied, 'for a little while.'

Her aunt fixed the tossed blankets and sheets some of which were hanging to the floor. She was bemused. All this mess and Nora lying there calmly as if she hadn't stirred all evening.

'You must have had a bad dream!' Molly joked.

'Oh, yeah ...' Nora stuttered. 'But I ... I don't remember what it was.'

'Would you take a cup of tea?'

'No, thanks,' she hesitated and spoke again. 'Is Jack really a bank robber and a murderer?'

Molly's eyes lost their light as she sat heavily on the bed.

'I can't believe he is,' she said. 'Whatever he's done, it's only because he thinks it's right.'

'But those Irregulars do terrible things,' Nora insisted. 'My father told me and I read it in the newspapers!'

'I know, I know but the Free State boys are no angels either,' Molly said and lowered her head into her hands, 'Look at me! Making excuses for killing and ...'

She looked as if she might burst into tears and Nora found herself comforting her.

'One thing is certain,' Molly murmured, 'that we women will be left picking up the pieces.'

Nora remembered her mother saying something similar not so long ago. She had the strangest feeling that her mother was there in the room, watching over them in their confusion. Molly blew her nose and took hold of herself.

'Nora, there's evil on both sides and good on both sides, but the longer it goes on the less good there is on either side,' she whispered. 'If you knew Jack, you couldn't imagine him doing the awful things that crowd get up to. You just couldn't.'

They heard Peter calling from the kitchen and as he mounted the stairs Molly hurriedly tucked the bedclothes around Nora and turned off the oil lamp.

'If he sees me in this state the poor man will be up the wall entirely,' she said. 'He's sick with worry but he's happy tonight and we don't want to spoil it for him, do we?'

'I suppose not,' Nora said, listening to him whistling his way up the stairs.

'Good night, girls!' he called and then whispered quietly, 'Oh, sorry. Is she asleep?'

'No, Peter, we were just having a bit of a chat,' Molly said, a little flustered.

'Is everything all right?'

Molly didn't answer and Nora guessed she wasn't able to.

'It is, Uncle Peter,' she piped up.

'Grand so,' he said. 'See you in the morning, then.'

Feeling closer to Molly than she'd ever imagined she would, the time seemed right to ask about something else that was on her mind. It had bothered her more and more as it became obvious that Molly was no ogre.

'Molly,' she asked, 'why did Mam never come back here and why did you never visit us in Inchicore?'

'All of that is best forgotten.'

'But I have to know.'

Molly took a while to consider whether she should answer. Her silence threatened to kill the goodwill between them.

'Our parents,' Molly said finally, 'had her life all planned out for her. Where she'd work, what kind of man she'd marry. Everything. They were like that. It didn't matter to them how you felt about it. They were very hard on her and she ran away to Dublin to have her own life.'

Nora found it hard to imagine that such an independent girl could have ended up as a slave to someone like her father.

'She wasn't long in Dublin,' Molly continued, 'when they both took ill in that awful flu epidemic. She came down but Mam died before she got here.'

'I'm sorry, Molly, you don't have to say any more.'

Her aunt was lost in the misery of those days.

'Poor Annie,' she said, shaking her head, 'she asked Dad to forgive her but he sent her away. He just wouldn't listen.'

'But *you* could have come to see us.' Nora declared.

'Oh, I went up there all right,' her aunt sighed, 'you were just a baby but she was so bitter and your father was so mad when he saw her get upset! They told me never to darken their door again. I used to write but I never got an answer. In the end, I suppose, I gave up and that's a thing I'll always regret.'

Molly didn't say so but Nora guessed that by taking care of her she was trying to make up for the years of silence.

'Just before she died she wrote to me. I was so happy when that letter dropped into the hall ... But, God, when I read it my heart was broken. I wanted to come up but she wouldn't have it. She said it would be too painful for the two of us.'

It seemed to Nora that her own life was a mirror of her mother's. The separation from her family, the cruel unforgiving father, the escape to another place. For her mother that place of escape had itself become a prison. She couldn't let that happen to her. As if she had guessed at what was going through Nora's mind, Molly reassured her.

'Don't ever think we'd keep you here against your will, Nora,' she said, 'if it comes to it and you want to go back to Dublin, we won't stand in your way. Your father will just have to cope as best he can.'

'I don't want to go back,' Nora told her. 'The boys will soon be gone anyway. There'll be nothing left then.'

'We'll make the best of it, girl,' Molly said finally. 'It mightn't turn out so bad.'

Left alone in her room Nora felt a twinge of guilt that she hadn't confided in Molly. Tired and sore, her mind began to fill with the sweet melody Alec Smithson had played earlier at Parnell Hall. A time would come, she imagined sleepily when all their troubles were over – her own, those of her brothers, Molly and Peter's, and Jack's troubles too. When that time came she would put aside her promise never to play the piano again. This would be the melody she would play and it would be the overture to all their new tomorrows.

Chapter 9

The following day Nora decided to keep watch on the off-chance that Jack was still around. What she'd do if he did show up she had no idea but she was nonetheless determined.

Her first problem was the struggle over and back to the window. She asked her aunt if the bed could be moved across there.

'That's where my bed was at home,' she explained. 'Beside the window. Would it be too much trouble?'

'Not at all,' Molly said and within the hour Peter had bundled the bed across the floor.

The day seemed to last forever as Nora waited impatiently for nightfall. Not even a book from her mother's shelves could occupy her mind. To make matters worse, as daylight began to fade, she had an unwelcome visitor.

Clean-shaven, his suit dusted off, Alec Smithson arrived to check on her progress. She threw her eyes to heaven when he burst good-humouredly into her room. He was a little taken aback by her reaction but laughed it off.

'Delighted to see me, as always.'

'You'd never think of knocking before you charge in, would you?'

'Excuse me, Madam!' he said and stepped back outside.

After a short pause he tapped lightly on the half-open door. Nora was seething with frustration by now and wondered how Molly and Peter could let this madman near her. The knocking went on and she tried to keep from yelling at him.

At the same time she knew that the only way to get rid of him quickly was to let him in so he could fix up her bandages and leave her to her vigil.

'Come in!' she called and this time he entered quietly. He seemed embarrassed by his earlier high spirits.

'If I offended you ...' he started but she told him it was all right. She didn't have time to be petulant.

As he went about unwrapping and tightening her bandages his gloved hands trembled and he apologised again and again for his clumsiness.

'Had a few too many last night, I'm afraid,' he laughed unconvincingly.

This stirred her once more and she suddenly felt less sorry for him than she had allowed herself to moments before.

'Why do you do things like that? Don't you know all the trouble it causes?' she snapped.

'I'm doing no harm to anyone only myself,' he said.

'What about your parents or your wife and children?'

'I'm not married and my mother and father gave up on me long ago.'

She knew she'd already said too much but it was difficult not to go on.

'What about yourself? Aren't you killing yourself!'

He smiled again and shook his head wearily.

'Wouldn't I be a great loss to humankind,' he replied and went back to fumbling with the bandages.

Only now did she notice that the middle finger of his left hand stuck straight out as he worked. The more she looked, the more she realised he couldn't bend it at all.

'What happened to your finger?' she asked with cool directness.

'Paralysed,' he said. 'Lucky the whole hand isn't gone.'

'Did you get shot?'

'No. I ... Look, will you please stop staring at my hands?' he burst out.

'Excuse me for living,' she exclaimed and suddenly remembering how beautifully he had played that melody, added, 'But how can you manage the piano?'

'There's always a way if you know you have to.'

She was just about to tell him that his playing seemed perfect to her ears when he spoke again. His words were a strange echo of Mrs Teehan's.

'Sometimes the music is all there is left to you.'

His work finished he stood up to go.

'Well, that's you fixed up for another while,' he said. 'Don't be trying to move around too much now.'

'How long before I can go downstairs, would you say?'

'I'm afraid you'll have to grin and bear it for a couple of weeks more.'

'What!' she cried. 'Is there nothing else you can do? I'll go mad up here.'

'Sorry, Nora,' he smiled but raising his stiff finger to his chin he went on, 'Maybe there is actually. A bit of a long shot, mind you, but you never know ...'

'Tell me. What is it?'

'When I lived in Paris,' Alec said, 'I had this African friend and ...'

'Was he black?' she asked, wide-eyed.

'Black as the ace of spades and a proper gentleman.'

'You never lived in Paris!' she said accusingly.

'Indeed I did,' he said. 'Studied music there for two years before the War, after I packed in the medicine. And gallivanted around it for another two years when the War was over.'

He looked at her sternly and placed the stiff finger to his mouth as she opened her mouth to speak.

'Now stop interrupting me. You asked me to try something else so let me get back to my friend. You see his father was what you might call a "medicine man" and he passed on his spells to his son and he passed them on to me.'

Nora was becoming worried and wondered whether he was serious or simply insane. He started up a most peculiar chant and flapped his arms like wings. She sat up and was about to shout at him to stop when she noticed a grin work its way across his face. All at once he broke into a fit of hysterical laughter.

'You believed me, didn't you?' he roared.

She grabbed the book she'd been leafing through and flung it at him. He ducked and dashed towards the door holding up the book as protection in case she should throw something else. From between its leaves a folded sheet of paper floated to the floor.

They both stared at it as if unsure whether he should pick it up. After a moment of silence he did just that. He opened out the page and his eyes, skimming across it, slowly lit up until he was grinning mischievously again.

'Nora! I'm surprised at you,' he exclaimed.

He began to read in a grand manner:

> *'To My Sweetheart*
> *We walked along towards Templemore*

On a sunlit day in Spring
And stopped a while in Morley's Wood
To hear the young birds sing ...'

His smile withered away. His eyes filled with shame as hers did with pain. They both guessed it must be a poem written long ago by Nora's mother. Alec folded the sheet and placed it in the book.

'I'm sorry.'

'Go away,' Nora's voice was cracking.

He left the book on the bed and went. Nora knew he would probably go and drink his shame away but she didn't care. It was all he deserved.

She tried to think of Jack and rekindle the excitement she'd felt earlier at her plan to keep watch for him. The vision of her mother, young and happy would not easily go away.

Outside the sky was clear and the moon full and bright. Bright enough to read her mother's poem by.

She flipped open the book and found the single loose sheet. In the moonlight it was no longer yellow and old but white as the day it was first written on. The writing was careful and precise, the letters perfectly formed. She read the poem through again and again. It didn't matter to her who the words were addressed to or even how embarrassing they seemed at first. What mattered was that they were her mother's words from a happier time.

To My Sweetheart
We walked along towards Templemore
On a sunlit day in Spring
And stopped a while in Morley's Wood
To hear the young birds sing.

And in amongst the budding trees
We found a cottage bare
And promised that one day we'd make
Our very own home there.

Her mother would never walk that road again, never hear those birds or make a home among those trees. For hours she waited by the window for Jack to come, reciting the poem until she knew it by heart. But he never came. Not that night, or the next and after a week she gave up and wondered why she had bothered in the first place.

Besides, she was improving more quickly than anyone had expected and soon she would be ready to descend the stairs to the world she had been cut off from for too long.

Chapter 10

'You can start,' Alec Smithson said, 'by walking around the room with this.'

Nora viewed the crutch apprehensively. It was an old wooden thing that had, by the worn look of it, seen one too many through their injuries. Alec could see she wasn't impressed.

'Sorry I couldn't get a better one,' he told her. 'Fact is, it's a souvenir from the Great War.'

He was still plainly mortified by his foolishness over the poem. Nora was prepared to enlist his help in getting back to normal but had no intention of forgiving him. She had decided to speak to him only when it couldn't be avoided. For the moment she dismissed every word he said with a contemptuous toss of her fair hair.

On her first few attempts at taking off on the crutch she fell back agonisingly on the bed. She felt ridiculous hopping up and down like a jack-in-the-box. Eventually, however, she managed to spring up and find her balance so that, at last, she was standing.

She moved slowly and shakily away from the safety of the bed, like a ship making its first voyage in the roughest of waters. Whenever she faltered, Alec was there to support her annoying her so much that her determination grew stronger by the minute.

'That's enough for now,' he said finally. 'You can try again tomorrow.'

She was glad to take a rest but happy to have made such progress, and certain that it would only be a matter of days before she took those steep stairs. It was hard to believe that only a few short weeks after walking so reluctantly into the shop and kitchen below she could now look forward so much to seeing them again.

She began to like the idea of helping out in the shop and doing her share of housework. It was what she was used to and at least here she wouldn't have to take all the responsibility as she had to during her mother's illness.

'You'll be flying it in no time,' Alec had said that first day with the crutch and this soon proved to be true.

The day she came out onto the landing and down to the hallway was something of a royal occasion. Not only were her aunt and uncle and Alec there but a handful of customers who happened to come into the shop were invited in to share the celebration. There was tea and a fruit cake Molly had made and smiles all round.

Her sudden shyness was forgotten in the pleasure of being fussed over. It reminded her of days at Mrs Teehan's when, after the lesson, she would bring tea and something sweet and they would talk. To be precise, Nora would listen, as Mrs Teehan spoke of the music she loved and the wonderful musicians and singers who came to Dublin when she was a girl. The exotic names meant nothing to Nora but it was good to relax and listen.

'You're very quiet in yourself,' Molly said when all the visitors had left.

'I'm fine,' she said. 'The cake was grand. Everything was.'

'Only what you deserve after all you've been through,' Peter said. 'Now, I think it's time to open up shop again. Maybe you'd like to come out there for a bit?'

Nora still didn't trust him, and suspected he knew more about Jack and the Irregulars than he pretended. However, the need for a break from the monotony of her room was stronger than any doubts she harboured.

She spent the afternoon and most of the following days and weeks behind the shop counter. She loved the homely, clean smell of the place. There was a kind of freshness about that mixture of odours that seemed to clear her head each time she stepped inside. Crisp-crusted bread; flour and oatmeal in spotlessly white canvas bags; the pure tang of paraffin oil; the rich, creamy scent of milk and home-made butter.

Peter showed her how to operate the silver cash-register until even with her right arm still in its sling, she could work it faultlessly with her left hand. Then there were all the little tasks you never knew about when you were on the other side of the counter — like checking the stock and knowing when this or that item needed to be ordered. There were prices to be learned: six pence for a quart of milk, nine pence for a bottle of sauce, two shillings for a tin of salmon.

There was also the important business of keeping an account of the customers' purchases. This was done in the 'tick book'. Some people paid at the end of the week, others whenever they had money. Nora realised as the weeks passed that there were more than a few who never paid at all. Yet she never once saw Peter refuse any of them.

Nora herself had known times when there was no money

to pay for even the few essentials. Her mother almost always found a way to pay off the bill and the local shopkeepers trusted her, but there were also times when even the most trusting would turn her away. Nora remembered when the railwaymen, not for the first time, had gone on strike for fair pay. She had known the humiliation of being refused a loaf of bread in the corner shop. Even to think of it now, after all this time, made her feel sick. Being on the inside of the counter, when stocks were low with the times that were in it, was something Nora could appreciate more than most.

Her respect for her uncle grew too, as she saw his foolhardy generosity and realised what it must mean to his customers who never had to leave empty-handed and feel, as she once did, that the world had no place at all for some.

When the shop was quiet she would read the newspapers to pass the time. The news was full of ambushes, gun battles and terrible killings. It seemed to confirm that she'd been better off not meeting Jack. Yet all these things were happening elsewhere — down in Cork or Kerry. Even those closer to home meant little to her since she had never heard of most of the villages and towns in the area.

Listening to customers talking to Peter in the shop she was reassured that the town was well-guarded by Colonel O'Brien's Free State soldiers. There was more worrying talk though about the spate of robberies locally in spite of the strong army presence. Most people, naturally, blamed the Irregulars but others had a different view of it.

'If you ask me,' one old woman said, as she stuffed her unpaid-for bread into her message bag, 'it's them soldiers are at it!'

'Now, Mrs Larkin,' Peter said, keeping up a cheerful front, 'don't you know as well as I do, the Colonel wouldn't stand for it.'

'Well, he can't be watching the whole lot of them all the time, can he?'

If all this seemed unimportant to Nora it was because she was beginning to feel contented in a way she could never have imagined. Her sling had been thrown off and though her arm was very stiff she was getting back the use of it. The crutch too was cast aside and she was able to move around even if it was a nuisance to have to dodder along so slowly.

From time to time she was left in charge of the shop when her uncle had business up the town and her aunt was busy making butter or baking in the kitchen. There was no question of her going to school just yet and in any case that great grey block of a place was home, for the present, to the new company of soldiers. Among them, she had heard Peter tell Molly darkly was the infamous Captain Doyle.

It didn't bother her that she couldn't yet go out and meet others of her own age. Making friends was difficult when you knew how easy it was to lose them.

There were other reasons for her to feel some satisfaction in her new surroundings. Her father's promise to send money to help with her keep had been playing on her mind. Somehow she felt he would find this promise easy to break. Yet, she dared to hope that he might choose not to forget. She thought that if he gave Molly and Peter even a little, it would make her feel less of a burden on them. It would even, perhaps, give her a sense of independence to think that she was paying her way.

Then one day as she settled out the morning papers on the counter a man wearing the familiar railway guard's hat came into the shop. He was about her father's age and his thick Dublin accent made her long for home and especially for her brothers.

'You're Nora Canavan, aren't you?' he inquired.

'I am,' she said. 'Who wants to know?'

'Jimmer Casey,' he said offering a friendly hand.

She stepped back from the counter in panic, certain he was coming with bad news, and called out, 'Aunt Molly.'

'Nora!' he cried, 'I'm only here to deliver ...'

'It's the lads, isn't it?' she murmured. 'They're gone. Or something terrible is after happening.'

Molly rushed in from the door behind her, red-faced from the heat of the kitchen.

'What's wrong, girl?'

'Mrs Delaney,' Jimmer laughed uneasily. 'She frightened the livin' daylights out of me!'

'Molly put her around Nora's shoulder.

'What do you want with us?' she said firmly.

He reached his hand inside his long coat and produced a letter.

'Jim Canavan asked me to give you this,' he said.

'For me, is it?' Nora said relieved.

'It's addressed to Mrs Delaney. There you are, ma'am.'

Nora hid her disappointment as Molly opened the letter. Reading through it, Molly smiled and finally put it in her apron pocket.

'It's just a few bob for your keep, Nora,' she said. 'And he's asking for you and says the boys are fine.'

It didn't seem possible that her father could ever make her happy but just this once he had. Molly lifted the end of the counter and asked Jimmer inside for a bite to eat.

'I'm fine, Missus,' he said. 'You're a busy woman, I'm sure.'

'Not too busy to let a man go all the way back to Dublin on an empty stomach.'

Jimmer's visits soon became a weekly occurrence and Nora looked forward to hearing his cheerful gossip from the

streets where she used to live. Whenever a name was mentioned she would explain to her aunt who the person was,
what they looked like and anything else she could remember
about them.

When a railway strike put a temporary halt to Jimmer's
weekly calls a cloud descended on her contentment. She
worried about the boys and actually wished that their tickets
would arrive for America soon. She even found herself feeling real concern for her father. To her astonishment and relief,
Peter put five pounds in the post and saw them through the
crisis.

In a few short weeks, Jimmer was back, cheerful as ever in
spite of the hard times he too must have experienced.

When this cloud had passed she discovered a new joy. It
came like a ray of sunshine — or a beam of starlight.

Her reluctance to go to the Stella Cinema had remained in
spite of her new-found appetite for living. She made all kinds
of excuses to convince herself that she wouldn't like it. The
crowds, she thought, would be unbearable. Besides, someone
might bump against her elbow or accidentally kick her ankle.

The films too, she imagined, would be nothing but roman-
tic nonsense or just plain silly. The truth was she was afraid
she really would enjoy it and this made her feel guilty. It
didn't seem right, so soon after her mother's death to let
herself surrender altogether to happiness. It was enough for
the moment to be as content as she was.

Every weekend she listened at her window to the cheering
and gasps of wonder. Most attentively of all, she listened to
Alec Smithson's piano. It became more and more difficult to
pretend to herself. She began to think that if she went there
just once, she might see what it was really like and never want
to go again.

In the end she knew that she would only give in if she had

to, if something happened that in some way compelled her to go.

Another Friday had arrived. Jimmer had come and gone for another week and Molly sat in the kitchen sneezing and shivering miserably. Nora was doing what she could of her aunt's work and there wasn't time even to consider that her opportunity might have arrived.

'It's the bed for you, Molly,' Peter said as he passed through the kitchen, busy with his usual preparations for the evening.

'But who'll take in the money and help you tidy up after?' Molly asked.

'I'll do it,' Nora spoke up.

They looked at her in astonishment. They had grown used to her excuses and had given up trying to persuade her to come. As in everything else they saw no point in forcing her and guessed that in time she would make up her own mind to take at least one excursion there. They hadn't expected it to be quite so soon.

'I'd be able to, no bother,' she said, worried that their silence betrayed some doubt.

'I'm sure you would,' Peter said at last. 'But would it be fair on you? It's hard going, you know.'

Nora looked pleadingly at Molly as Peter considered the matter. Before long he relented.

'Well, you've had plenty of practice in the shop. So, I suppose ...'

'Thanks,' Nora enthused, 'I won't make any mistakes.'

'And what harm if you do,' Molly sniffled.

After tea, Molly went to bed and Nora went out through the back yard and across the lane to the hall with Peter. Her slight limp had almost disappeared by now and by the time they reached the door, she'd forgotten all about it.

Peter brought her to the little room at the entrance which had a small window where people passed in their coins and got their tickets in return. He showed her the cash-box with its drawers for shillings, tanners, threepenny bits, pennies, halfpennies and farthings.

Then there were the rolls of tickets. One small roll of pink ones were for the small balcony. Two larger rolls of white tickets with '6d' printed on them were for the adults in the main hall. The last roll was coloured green and were the children's tickets, up the front. They were marked with a bold '3d'.

'You might find a few of the older lads looking for the green ones,' he warned, 'but if there's any problem, call Alec. He'll be at the front door. They're all afraid of him. God knows why!'

He saw that she was beginning to grow pale and that her hands were none too steady.

'The big thing to remember,' he advised, 'is to take your time and Alec will close the door when he thinks there's enough of them inside. Then you can relax and I'll take the cash up the back with me.'

In the confined space she kept herself busy arranging and rearranging her chair until she found she could comfortably reach the small window which Peter had slid open. She went through the task ahead over and over again in her mind. Soon, the first coin rolled on to the small window-ledge.

'A threepenny!' the tiny squeak of a voice cried.

She looked up but could see no face. A black-gloved hand appeared at the window and she knew it was Alec Smithson. His alcohol-stained breath filled her nostrils and she flinched away in disgust.

'You're nothing but a dirty oul' drunk,' she snapped but he was gone.

She listened as he fumbled with the door to the street and yelled out, 'Will ye take yere time? We're not starting for another hour.'

Nora was soon too busy with the pink, white and green tickets to bother about him after that. The crowds poured in and every once in a while Peter came in to give her a helping hand. Her right arm was aching but she was too excited with all the activity to let it stop her. It was such a change from the quiet days in her room that by the time Alec had closed the front door she was in a daze.

Peter came and collected the cash-box and they went into the hall. The audience waited impatiently for the show to begin. A loud cheer and wild whistling greeted Peter as he made his way onto the stage. He raised his hand and in a few moments there was something like silence.

'Tonight's pictures are,' he announced, '*The Mistress of Shenstone* with Pauline Frederick and *Black is White*, starring Dorothy Watson.'

The roar of the crowd was ear-splitting. Peter yelled cheerfully from the stage but to no avail. He folded his arms and waited for quiet to descend once more. At last, he was able to continue.

'Now, a warning to you boyos down the back,' he called. 'No firing apple butts at each other.'

After another cacophony of noise he was allowed to speak again.

'And you boyos up the front! No firing butts at Mr Smithson!'

Alec stood up from behind the little three cornered screen surrounding his piano and took an exaggerated bow. He raised the white broad-brimmed hat from his head just in time to receive an apple butt on the ear. He glared maliciously at the rows of children and warned:

'One more assault on my person and I'm off.'

Someone called from the balcony, 'I seen the lad who done that and if he do it again he won't mind my cattle at the Fair next week.'

It took several more minutes for order to be restored. Nora couldn't help wishing she could have thrown that butt at Alec.

'Serves him right!' she thought, as the lights went down and the first film started. She found herself swept along by the story of the *Mistress of Shenstone*, living every scene of hard times and heartbreak and applauding with all the others, her salvation from tyranny. All the while, Alec in spite of the fact that he must certainly have been drinking before the show, played with a feverish intensity.

During the second film an old man, seeing the villain sneak up behind the hero, roared, 'Look ahind you! Look ahind you!'

The laughter that followed was infectious. There were some quieter moments too, when the hero and heroine were together. Nora hated these bits except for the fact that Alec played that same haunting tune.

She wondered if she was capable of playing it even if her arm had completely healed. Indeed, she was thinking the same of all the bits and pieces he went through during the two hours. In the end, however, she could not shake off the feeling that no good would come of returning to the piano. It had hastened her mother's death, drawn her father's wrath down on her and broken up her family.

Even Alec, who could play so perfectly despite his wounds, was an alcoholic wreck. This was more proof if she needed it of the hopelessness of having musical talent. Perhaps it made other people happy to listen like this crowd had, like Mrs Teehan had once done. This was little consolation, she thought, compared to the misery it brought upon the player. All in all, it was better to sit back and let someone else do the thankless job of making music.

After the crowd had gone, there was the tidying up to do and Nora's mood improved again. It had been an enjoyable night and she had no doubt but that she wanted to come to every show now.

And so she did. Friday night became the high-point of her week. There was always something new to make her laugh or to surprise her. Until a night came when her sense of wonder turned to shock and the happy days changed to dangerous, even murderous ones.

Chapter 11

It had been another wild night at the Stella Cinema. Peter's dire warnings had, as usual, been ignored by the rowdy element. Apple butts had flown and Alec had threatened once more to lock up the piano and leave. But it was all good-humoured madness and Nora had to admit to herself that Alec had truly excelled himself.

The melody, now imprinted on her mind, had never sounded sweeter. She hummed it quietly while she swept the hall floor when suddenly she hit upon what made it so perfect. If you were sad, the thing matched your mood but if you were happy it suited just as well. That seemed to be the secret to its strange hold over her.

At eleven o'clock Peter locked up the hall behind them and he and Alec and Nora headed back to the house. A light frost and a full moon above gave the cobbles in the yard a magical sparkle. The cloudless sky was studded with stars. Alec noticed how she stared at them and raised his eyes too.

'They'll all be there when we're long gone,' he said.

Peter shrugged his shoulders.

'Ah, it's a great night. Isn't that all that matters now?' he declared.

Nora knew that each was right in his own way. In any case she felt that nothing could intrude on the warm feeling inside her, not even the sharp, frosty air. When they reached the house she reluctantly went inside.

In the kitchen they sat and drank the tea Molly had prepared for them. Alec was delighted to be told time and again by Peter how well he'd performed. As far as Peter was concerned he'd made the pictures seem much better than they really had been.

'I think the first one was a bit of a dud.' he said.

'*The Bell That Never Rang* is right,' Alec laughed. 'And it didn't ring tonight either!'

They all joined in his laughter except Nora, though she was tempted to. She wouldn't forget his thoughtlessness so easily. She thought about the stars and wished she could go outside again.

'Holy God!' Peter exclaimed. 'I left the film rolls in the hall!'

'I'll get them,' Nora offered, jumping to her feet.

'But it's too late for you to be out,' Molly told her.

'I don't mind. And it's a lovely night.'

'Take the lamp then,' Peter said, 'and mind you don't let it fall.'

Outside, everything was lit so clearly by the moon that it was more like early morning than midnight. She went quickly to the hall, hurrying in to get the rolls of film, so she could stroll back and watch the sky again. She returned by the lane and stood in the yard beside one of the outhouses. Watching her warm breath rise towards the sky she raised her head as far back as it would go, to see as many stars as she possibly could.

The face appeared behind her just as a cold, damp hand fastened itself over her mouth. She was dragged back into the outhouse and the door closed before her, locking away the stars.

'I don't want to hurt you,' the stranger's voice whispered.

She swung her arms and tried to kick the door but he pulled her back from it.

'Please, don't struggle. Just listen to me for a minute.'

She waited to hear what he had to say only slightly reassured by the tremor in his voice.

'My name is Jack,' he said. 'Peter's brother.'

She wasn't surprised but her fear remained.

'I'm going to take my hand away now,' he said, 'and I won't ask you not to scream. I'll leave it up to yourself.'

He withdrew his hand and she jerked herself away from him.

'What do you want from me?' she asked fearfully.

'I'm sick,' he told her, 'and I need to lay up here for a bit. Will you help me?'

She heard him slide down the wall and slump in the straw at her feet.

'You're a murderer,' she said evenly, 'and a bank robber and wasn't it you who tried to break into my room. Why should I help you?'

'No reason at all, I suppose,' he said weakly. 'But I'm not any of those things, only fighting for what's right. What I think is right, anyway.'

'Wasn't there peace until the likes of you started at it again?'

She realised he hadn't the strength to stop her walking out whenever she chose to. Nothing was stopping her. Nothing except his obvious weakness and the sincerity of his denials. She remembered too Molly's words.

'If you only knew Jack, you couldn't believe such things of him.'

'What can I do? I ...' she began but his hushed voice stopped her dead. 'You sound very like your mother,' he said, 'Only for that oul' Dublin accent.'

'There's nothing wrong with my accent!' she said angrily, thinking he had a nerve to ask favours and throw out an insult in the next breath.

'Divil a bit wrong with it. Some of my best friends have the same affliction.'

'Why don't you ask them to help you so?'

'No-one knows I'm here only yourself. All I want is a blanket and some food.'

'And if you're caught,' she objected, 'I'll get the blame. I could go to jail.'

'I wouldn't mention your name,' he promised.

'Can't you just go in and ask your brother? He's probably mixed up with you fellows too.'

'I'll have nothing to do with him. He should be out leading us,' he said shakily. 'Anyway, I don't want to bring trouble on him, for Molly's sake.'

'But you'd bring it on me.'

'Nobody would suspect you.'

She could sense, even in darkness, that he was giving up on her. He breathed out a long, rasping, sickly sigh and tried as best he could to smother an agonising cough that shook through his body.

'It wasn't fair to ask you,' he said, at last. 'I don't know what I was thinking of.'

Just then there came a call from the house.

'Nora!'

It was Molly. She had looked out the back door and noticed to her horror the oil lamp and film rolls Nora had left on the ground as she gazed at the stars.

'Don't tell them,' he pleaded as she swung the door open and stepped out in the yard. Molly had gone back inside. Nora had just closed the door behind her when Peter came rushing out.

'Where in the name of God did you get to?' he thundered. 'Your aunt is in a state over you.'

'There was a cat in the lane,' she lied, fearing he would react like her father might in similar circumstances. 'I tried to catch it so I could give it some milk ... but it ran off.'

'Tell her you're sorry, will you?' he asked to her relief.

They went inside and her aunt was at the sink, pretending to be busy with the washing-up. Alec had already gone.

'I'm an awful fuss-pot.' she said.

'No, it was my fault,' Nora admitted. 'I won't let it happen again.'

Nothing more was made of it. Nora knew she could have explained everything by telling the truth but she needed time to decide what to do.

It proved to be a long sleepless night as she thought it all over. Whenever she came to a firm decision to let them know about Jack, she imagined him out there in the cold outhouse, sick and helpless. If she convinced herself that he was an evil and dangerous man, his weak voice came to her, filled with desperation.

After long hours of torment she was left without an answer to her problem. The only light in that troubled darkness for her was the certainty that Peter wasn't involved with the Irregulars. It was with this small comfort that she eventually found sleep.

Molly woke her at noon the following day. As they spoke, Nora wished she could ask her advice. She had come to trust her aunt and saw more and more of her mother in the woman

—her cheerful dedication to the work of the house and shop, the way she hummed to herself all the time, her concern for Nora and her devotion to her husband. The difference was that Peter returned this devotion and they seemed to share their tasks gladly.

'There was another robbery in town last night,' Molly told her and Nora's stomach sank.

She had spent the whole night thinking of him wasting away outside while, in all likelihood, he had simply been lying low in preparation for another raid. It made no sense to her that he should have shown himself at all. Whatever his reasons, she felt cheated, because during the long night her sympathy had grown in spite of her misgivings.

'I suppose it was the Irregulars,' she said bitterly. 'And that Jack fellow.'

Molly sighed and nodded her head in resignation.

'How can a man change so much?' she wondered aloud. 'He's just another gangster now like all the rest of them.'

Still Nora didn't tell her about Jack. Now, however, her only reason was to cover up her own foolishness for believing he was sick.

The shop kept her busy for the afternoon. She resisted the temptation to go and look in the outhouse. There could be no question but that he was gone by now. Even to consider any other possibility was ridiculous.

The temptation, however, refused to go away. When the shop closed for the evening she found herself, almost against her will, standing before the outhouse once again.

Light poured in to the straw-covered floor as she eased back the door. She was rocked on her heels by the putrid smell of vomit from inside. Just as she began to shut the door she saw the ragged bundle of a body in the far corner. It was difficult to speak without breathing in the foul air.

'Are you all right?' she gasped.

'I am,' Jack answered quietly.

There was no pretence here. Looking more closely she saw how he shook uncontrollably and how the feverish sweat wet his forehead.

'You can't stay in here,' she whispered. 'There must be somewhere you can go.'

'Believe me, I'd be gone long ago if I was able to stir.'

'But Peter will smell this awful ...' she began but was suddenly struck by an idea.

Under the stage in the Parnell Hall, she remembered, was a small door leading into a space that went right back to the end wall. She had opened it once and seen that it was full of broken old chairs and tattered curtains. No-one seemed to use it any more and it seemed to her a safer and warmer place for him to hide.

'I don't know,' he said when she told him of this hide-away. 'Peter is in and out of there a lot and then there's the shows.'

'You might be all right before Friday,' she said, hoping this would be the case. 'It's the only thing I can think of.'

Jack considered his situation for a moment and Nora waited, looking anxiously towards the house.

'You're right,' he agreed. 'Another night in this hole and I'm done for.'

'When it gets dark I'll bring the key and some food,' she said. 'Now I'll have to go back inside. They'll be wondering what I'm at.'

He took her hand and raised his tired eyes to her face. His square jaw was rough with bristle, his skin weather-beaten like one who had spent too much time out under the elements. If he had ever been young and carefree it no longer showed except in his eyes. They were, she now noticed, a paler, clearer blue than she'd ever seen. Without them he would have seemed ugly.

'You're the image of your mother,' he said. 'The other night when I saw you at the window, I got such a fright.'

'How do you think I felt?' she said uncomfortably.

'I don't know what I was thinking of, tramping up the stairs like that. I'm sorry.'

'And so you should be!'

'It broke my heart when I heard she was gone,' Jack whispered. 'Poor Annie.'

She released her hand. Her cheeks were flushed and she wasn't quite sure why.

'I really have to go.'

'Thanks, girl. I knew you wouldn't let me down.'

Later, as the evening set in she sneaked into the kitchen when her aunt and uncle were in the store. She cut some beef and thick slices of bread. She found an old pitcher and filled it with milk.

Out in the corridor she carefully took down the hall key from the rack on the coatstand and went softly to the back door and the yard.

The milk splashed over the rim of the pitcher and on to her clothes but there wasn't time to worry about that. She opened the outhouse door and called in a hushed voice. Jack struggled to his feet and came rather shakily into view. He faltered and she had to slip the food into her apron pocket so she could reach around his waist to support him. He leaned on her shoulder, apologising for being a nuisance and for putting her in danger. She got him inside the hall and into the new hideout.

'I'll come whenever I can,' she said. 'Here's some food and milk.'

Jack wrapped a heavy curtain around his shoulders and

laughed hoarsely, 'I always wanted to be on the stage but I never thought I'd end up under it.'

'I'm off,' Nora told him. 'I hope they're still in the store.'

'I'll be out of here as soon as I can stay on my feet and I won't trouble you any more,' Jack promised.

She closed the door on him and locked up the hall quickly. At the house she heard Molly and Peter talking in the kitchen. Slipping the key on its rack she stepped stealthily up the stairs. Her aunt called.

'Is that you, Nora?'

She turned and went back down the hallway, searching her mind for excuses. At the kitchen door she stood frozen to the spot. Sitting between Molly and Peter at the table was Colonel O'Brien and when he looked up he wasn't smiling.

Chapter 12

The blood drained from Nora's face. She reached out to the dresser to steady herself. With three pairs of eyes fixed on her, she was sure her guilty secret was out.

'Nora,' Molly said, 'you look like you've seen a ghost.'

Words refused to form in her mouth. Peter was on his feet and beside her in an instant. She cowered back and held her arm above her head. He stared, perplexed, at the girl.

'In the name of God,' he said, 'you don't think I'd hit you!'

'I'm sorry. I got such a fright.'

Colonel O'Brien moved in his chair and coughed uneasily.

'It's probably just the uniform,' he said, 'I don't blame her for being frightened.'

Somehow the atmosphere seemed to have lightened. She found her voice again.

'I was coming down the stairs and I tripped in the dark,' she told them, the lie coming very easily. 'I thought I'd fall the whole way down.'

'Sit down there,' Peter said, 'and I'll pour you a cup of tea.

That'll do the trick.'

She listened and said very little herself as they talked. There was something not quite right about this conversation. Seconds, sometimes minutes, passed while they searched desperately for something else to say. Peter and Molly seemed to be watching the clock on the dresser too often.

There was no doubt that her aunt and uncle actually liked the Colonel and that he liked them but something was getting in the way of this friendship. It didn't take a lot of figuring out to guess that Jack was the cause of this tension.

After half an hour the Colonel got up to leave and Molly and Peter saw him to the front door. Nora gathered up the cups and saucers and went about washing up. When she'd finished she heard the three of them talking quietly. She went to the half-open door and listened.

'Look, Peter,' the Colonel said, 'he's definitely back in the area somewhere. I'm not saying he's caught up in the robberies but some of those boys are.'

'The last I heard was he'd gone to Limerick but that was a few months ago,' Peter said, exasperation shaking his voice. 'How can they get in around the town with all the men you have here?'

'I know, I know, it shouldn't happen,' Colonel O'Brien agreed. 'If you ask me there's too many coincidences in all this. Every time they strike my lads seem to be somewhere else and it's all Captain Doyle's fault as far as I can see.'

'People are starting to say it's your own men who're at it,' Molly told him.

'It's a possibility I have to consider. In fact I've already been looking into it and between ourselves I'm beginning to think there may be a few bad apples on both sides in on it. All I have though is the one clue. This piece of spectacle lens and it's got me nowhere.'

'I'll tell you the truth,' Peter confided. 'If it had just been one raid I'd be certain it was the Irregulars alone. I mean they have to have money for guns and supplies. But there's been too many of them. All that cash is lining someone's pocket, I'll wager.'

'If I could only talk to Jack,' the Colonel sighed. 'I've had word there'll be an amnesty announced soon. All they have to do is hand over the guns and the past will be forgotten.'

'You know you can trust me,' Peter told him. 'If I get even an inkling of where he is, I'll do my level best to get the two of you together.'

'You're a decent man, Peter,' Colonel O'Brien said finally. 'I can't ask any more of you. For God's sake, be careful of this Doyle fellow, won't you. I can't guarantee he'll leave you in peace when I'm out of town.'

Listening to their goodbyes, Nora began to dry the delph. She stayed only a short while after Molly and Peter returned to the kitchen. The hushed conversation at the front door had given her even more pause for thought. Gazing across at the hall from the window of her room, she thought of Jack sleeping off his fever unaware of the Colonel's visit. She would try to persuade him to take up the amnesty offer when she got a chance to sneak over there the next day. The Colonel was a man who could be trusted she was sure and Jack must have known that too.

Jack and Peter were once young and innocent just like her own brothers. She wondered if it wasn't for the best, after all, that the boys should go away from this troubled country where brothers took different sides and came to detest each other. It almost made the prospect of their going a bearable one. In any case there was little time for sad foreboding. The all-too-real adventure that lay before her put paid to that.

Morning when it came brought another unexpected surprise.

Before she opened her eyes she was aware of a strange brightness. She sat up to the window and saw that the yard and outhouses, the lane and further away, the Parnell Hall — everything, as far into the distance as she could see — was covered in a thick blanket of snow.

The vast sweep of whiteness seemed to make the world clean and pure. When she remembered Jack the harsh reality of the cold made her shiver. She wished she could be a child again and enjoy the wonder and excitement of such days. Right now, staring lazily at the day was simply a waste of precious time.

Her first concern was to come up with an excuse to go to the hall. Then there was the problem of getting more food and drink for Jack. Cold milk and bread would be of little use to him after such a freezing night.

By the time she'd reached the kitchen a plan was already forming in her mind. When Molly asked what she'd like for breakfast she pretended not to be hungry and took only a slice of bread with her tea. Then she made a big show of asking if she could go out the back and play in the snow. Molly was more than happy to let her go and enjoy herself. She saw this as yet another sign that Nora was settling down well and coming to terms with her great loss.

'Would you not prefer to play on the street?' Molly suggested. 'You never know but you might meet a new friend.'

'No,' she answered, 'I'd prefer to be on my own.'

Molly didn't push her any further. Nora went and took down the key, praying that no-one would notice it was missing. She wrapped up well and went outside.

Her shoes crunched ankle-deep into the icy snow and only when she was already half-way across the yard did she realise that her's were the sole footprints there. It was a strangely breath-taking feeling to look around at those small, short, steps leading to where she stood now and at the unspoiled whiteness before her.

Strange it was because she couldn't help thinking that the snow-crushed trail was in some way not hers at all. Breathtaking too because the huge uncharted, bright space beyond seemed to suggest that the whole world was hers and that wherever she went she would leave her mark.

She ran to the end of the yard and began to gather snow as if she was about to build a snowman. Suddenly, she dashed away to the hall, unlocked it but left the door closed and returned to the house.

To her consternation, Peter was standing at the coatstand searching through the pockets of his own and Molly's coats. The object of his search was still burning into Nora's palm.

'Did you see the key to the hall, Nora?' he asked scratching his head. 'I'm sure I left it on the rack.'

She walked over as calmly as she could to the coatstand.

'No,' she lied, 'maybe it fell down below.'

'I don't think so. I've already tried.'

She got down on her hands and knees and struggled in beneath the hems of the heavy coats.

'I'm telling you, Nora,' he told her, 'it's not there!'

'Here it is!' she exclaimed, slipping the key from her pocket.

So carried away was she that she banged her head against the corner of the coatstand as she stood up.

'By God! I must be blind as a bat,' he laughed.

Her head ached but she had to find out quickly why he wanted the key.

'Are you going over to the hall?' she asked.

'No. I just noticed it wasn't there when I hung up my coat.'

He went away to the shop with the newspaper packages he'd just collected from the railway station. It was time to put the rest of her plan into action. She climbed the stairs and found Molly tidying the rooms.

'Do you need a hand?' she asked.

'Not at all. Go out and enjoy yourself, it'll soon be melted away.'

'Could I put on a few sausages?' Nora said calmly. 'I'm starving.'

'I'll cook them for you, girl.'

'I'd like to do it myself. Would you mind?'

'I've plenty to do here anyway. But be careful and don't let the frying pan get too hot.'

It didn't take long to fry the sausages but finding an old teapot that Molly didn't use was more difficult. Eventually she came across one behind the saucepans under the dresser. She made the tea, wrapped sausages and bread in some greaseproof paper and grabbing a mug from the shelf stalked through the corridor again.

Stealing across the yard she could only hope that Molly wouldn't be passing by any of the back windows and notice her heading for the hall. The pattern of steps already leading there reminded her that she'd better have another excuse prepared in case someone mentioned it later.

At the door of the hall she dared to look back towards the house. There was no sign that she'd been seen. She slipped inside and it was as if she'd walked into a wall of ice. The place was much colder than she'd expected. Colder, by far, than it was in the open air.

She put the food down near the small trapdoor and pulled it open. At least there was no reek of vomit as there had been in the outhouse.

'Jack,' she whispered into the darkness and there was no reply.

'Jack!' she repeated anxiously and again no answer came.

She felt a great anger sweep through her. After all the risks she had taken, how could he have left without even a word of thanks? She went inside to make certain. It was impossibly dark and there was no sound but her own awkward fumbling through the broken chairs.

She called out his name but there seemed no point in continuing. On her knees she crawled back towards the chink of light at the door. Pushing chairs roughly out of her way she lost her balance and began to topple over. Her fingers plunged on to the soft bundle of a torn old stage-curtain.

The dusty air was filled with a small, animal-like croak. She waited in horror for the sinister patter of something scurrying away. There was no such noise. All at once, Nora knew it had to be Jack. She found his soaking forehead with her hand. She touched his frozen cheeks and moving her fingers to his mouth felt only the slightest hint of a breath.

'Jack!' she cried. 'Please wake up. Please!'

He didn't stir but the horrifying moan came again and again as she shook him violently, to no avail. All of this was too familiar to her. The sickly smell, the fever, the shallow breathing. She was filled again with the emptiness of her mother's absence. Alone and afraid, she couldn't think what to do, couldn't think at all. She took his hand and sat in despair listening to him struggle to draw life from the musty air all around them.

Chapter 13

How long she'd spent there paralysed with fear she had no idea. The earlier sense of urgency returned to her very slowly until, at last, she found herself taking stock of the situation. She decided to drag him across to the door and see if the sharper air in the hall might fill his weak lungs with a new vitality.

In the cramped space, she sweated and strained to move the dead-weight of his body. Her elbow troubled her and her ankle felt as if the ice had gone clear through her skin and wrapped itself around the bones. When she stopped to rest she thought that Molly and Peter would surely come upon them soon. At that moment it didn't seem to matter any more. She was going to have to give the game away now if only to save Jack's life.

With one last, super-human effort she got him to the door. In the light his face was a harrowing sight. Under his eyes were heavy dark circles. Cold drops of moisture glistened on his dark eyebrows and along the creased lines of his hollow cheeks. If it hadn't been for his lank red hair he might easily have been taken for a sixty-year-old.

She poured some tea into the mug she'd brought and waited for it to cool before pressing it to his lips. It trickled down his cheeks like muddy-brown tears.

Back in among the chairs she found another heavy curtain and wrapped him up well in it. She left the door slightly ajar and found her way dizzily out into the yard. So weak was she that she had difficulty keeping to the straight path of her own trail in the snow.

There seemed no choice left to her in the face of Jack's illness. She would have to break her word to him. Not to do so would almost certainly lead to his death. Peter would find a doctor for him and even if this meant Jack would, without a doubt, be captured it would be better than dying in that tomb-like space. He would be safe in Colonel O'Brien's hands — though she found reasons to doubt even this.

In the newspapers she had read more and more of Irregulars being executed by the government. She had never before doubted that these men were guilty of whatever crimes they were charged with. What, however, if it was true what some people were saying, that these men were simply being made examples of. Or perhaps there were those like Captain Doyle whom even the Colonel could not trust. Might he not extract vengeance before Jack ever got to trial.

'I have to get a doctor,' she repeated weakly to herself as she neared the back door of the house.

And then the possibility of an answer struck her. Alec Smithson. When she'd been hurt, Molly and Peter hadn't sent for a doctor. In fact, Molly had said that Alec was better than any doctor. He had fixed Nora up. Maybe, if he could be convinced, he could do the same for Jack. She would have to talk to him in spite of the business with the poem; there were more important things than pride. There was a chance that he'd refuse to help an Irregular and perhaps go to the military. It was a risk she would have to take.

In the shop, Peter sat behind the counter doing the books. She tried to hide the grimace of pain and guilt that threatened to overwhelm her.

'Well, are you having a good time out there?' he smiled.

'Yeah ... it's grand,' she said, wondering how she would go about finding out where Alec lived. She cursed herself for never having thought to ask before. There was only one way to approach it. The situation was too urgent for beating around the bush.

'Where is Alec's house?' she asked as nonchalantly as possible.

'Alec?' he said surprised, 'and why would you want to know that?'

'I don't know,' she mumbled. 'It was just that I never heard him talk about where he lived. I was curious.'

Peter put down his pen and rested his chin on his upturned hand.

'Poor old Alec,' he began. 'Well, he's not from these parts, you know. He's down from Birr side and to tell you the truth I don't think his people have much time for him.'

'But where does he stay?'

'He's above in Church Street at Mrs Roche's rooms,' Peter explained. 'That is, when he's sober and he's paid the rent. He sleeps rough some of the time. In fact, if I'm not mistaken, he was in one of our outhouses the other night.'

She turned quickly away to hide her blushes. Hearing Alec blamed for fouling up the outhouse made her feel even worse about concealing the truth from Peter. Surely, she thought, he was not the kind of man who would betray his own brother. She was almost moved to tell him everything but his words broke her resolve.

'You know, it's a terrible thing to say,' he sighed, 'but I often think Alec, for all his faults, is more of a brother to me than Jack ever was. There's ten years between us and that's an awful big gap.'

Nora shook her head in disbelief. There was six years between her and the two boys. She had never considered that it made any difference to the way she felt about them. Yet, when she thought about it, she realised that she had managed to survive without them and even begun to enjoy life again. Until Jack came along.

'I'm sorry, Nora,' Peter apologised. 'It just seems that way at times.'

He went back to his accounts and Nora paced around impatiently for what seemed like an eternity though the clock said only five minutes.

'Aunt Molly said I could play on the street,' she said finally. 'Would that be all right?'

''Course it would,' he said, cheerful again. 'Stay out as long as you like. You couldn't ask for healthier weather.'

The snow was turning to slush now under the midday sun, as she walked the short distance to Church Street. There, she asked a well-dressed young man where Mrs Roche's house was. He pointed disdainfully at an untidy-looking shambles of a building, squatting between two freshly painted houses.

She went and knocked at the door whose ancient green paint was blistered. Great dirty flakes of the stuff crunched beneath her feet. The door swung back and a big broad-shouldered woman with long strings of greasy-grey hair hanging from her chin grunted at her.

'What do you want?'

'I ... I was wondering ...' Nora stuttered, overcome by the woman's bulk.

'Speak up, girl,' the bearded woman bawled. 'I can't hear a word you're saying.'

'Is Mr Smithson at home, Missus?' Nora asked fearfully.

'Mr Delaney is looking for him, I suppose. No-one else in their right minds would bother with that waster!' she thundered so that the whole street could hear and then peering down suspiciously at Nora, asked, 'And who would you be now?'

'I'm ... I'm ...'

'Holy God!' the woman cried, 'You're Annie's daughter, God bless you!'

In an instant her stern look had faded to a tearful, almost tender, smile.

'Annie Hickey's daughter! I should have known. Aren't you the dead spit of her.'

'Is he in?' Nora asked with growing impatience.

'There's only one place you'll find the likes of him now,' the woman said, 'and that's over there in Donnelly's Public House and Mr Delaney should know better than to send a nice young one like yourself looking for him.'

'Thanks, Missus!' Nora said less than politely and dashed away leaving Mrs Roche tut-tutting behind her.

Donnelly's pub was empty when she lifted the latch and stepped inside. She hoped no-one else besides the bearded woman had seen her go in.

'Hello ...' she called.

Her stomach turned with the stale stench that seemed to cling to the very fabric of her clothes. She felt unclean. A bald head emerged from below the bar counter as if its owner had been hiding beneath it. The man sported a black moustache that was so large on his small face it didn't seem real. He looked for all the world like a character from one of the pictures she'd seen at the Stella Cinema.

She stifled a guilty laugh and pretended to cough. She waited for him to stand up and suddenly realised he was already on his feet.

'Can I help you, Miss?' he asked, his deep voice so out of place that she looked around to see if someone else had spoken.

'I'm looking for Mr Smithson,' she explained.

'He's not here,' the man said. 'At least he was but he went out and he came back in but I went down to the cellar and he was gone again, so I think he must be ... somewhere else, I suppose.'

Nora glared at the man with fire in her eyes. He was wasting her time. And Jack's. She turned to go and he started to ramble on again.

'Well, he could be out the back or he might be on his way in but I don't think so 'cause I was up the yard before I went down the cellar and he wasn't there but he might have been in here while I was out there and then when I came in he might have ...'

From behind a glass door to her left there came a knock to interrupt his pointless flow of words.

'Wait now,' the man whispered conspiratorially. 'There's someone in the snug.'

He crossed behind the counter to the other side of the partition and she heard a muffled conversation. She was beginning to feel her plan was all a big mistake when the man returned. Silently he jerked his thumb in the direction of the glass door.

She passed quietly in to the snug. Alec sat hunched over a low table. In his wavering hand he held a half-empty glass of stout. He raised one beady eye and his head rolled with the effort of keeping it fixed on her.

He sniggered so roughly that her skin crawled to think

how alcohol could change a man utterly. Even if he had been insensitive about the poem she knew there was some decency in him. Now he was exactly like her father in his worst moments. It seemed hopeless even to begin explaining what she wanted. That this miserable human being should be Jack's last fading hope of life drove her into a fit of rage.

She drew up her fist and with all the anger and bitterness of months, of years tearing at her heart she punched him squarely on the jaw. The glass fell from his gloved hand and he rocked back in his chair so hard that it went from under him. He collapsed in a drunken heap on the floor. Nora held her elbow and groaned with pain. The little moustached man appeared at the bar.

'What in the name of all that's holy's going on in here?' he bellowed.

Nora, still white with rage and hurt, looked fiercely at him. He ducked away preferring not to know what had happened. When he was out of sight he piped up.

'You'll pay for that glass, Smithson or you'll never get another bottle of stout in here!'

'Go 'way and wax your 'oul moustache, Baldy Conscience!' Alec yelled back at him from beneath the bench where he'd rolled.

Nora stood over him with her hands on her hips. If he was sober enough to answer the little man back, she thought, there might be some chance after all. She glared down pitilessly at him.

'Get up off the ground!' she ordered, her anger blocking any fear she might have had that he'd attack her.

'Where'd you learn to box like that?' he said with a wry smile and wiped away a trickle of blood from his mouth. The red streak it left across his cheek made him seem even more revolting than before.

'I need your help,' she told him firmly.

'And I need yours,' he replied, extending his hand. 'Give us a lift up.'

'You'll belt me.'

'I never hit a lady in my life,' he told her, 'bad and all as I am.'

She helped him to his feet. He held on the table unsteadily.

'That was an awful thing to do to a man.'

'You call yourself a man!' she answered indignantly. 'Stuck in a pub in the middle of the day and people dying ... *dying* because of you.'

He stared at her incredulously.

'What are you talking about, girl?'

'I'm talking,' she shouted and then realising the little man was more than likely listening to her every word, whispered, 'I'm talking about Jack.'

'Jack? Who the hell is Jack?'

'Will you keep your voice down,' she snarled. 'Jack Delaney, Peter's brother, the Irregular.'

She came closer hoping he wouldn't change his mind about hitting her.

'He's above in the Parnell Hall and he's barely able to breathe. I don't know what to do.'

Steering her towards the door, Alec took some change from his pocket and banged it on the counter.

'There's the money for your filthy glass, you miser!' he shouted and led her through to the street.

The warm sun had taken the sting out of the crisp air. Everything began to look ordinary again as the snow melted. Slush trickled into the gutter as they stood facing each other on the footpath.

'I suppose,' Nora said, 'you'll give the game away on Jack now.'

'I'll help any man who's sick, girl. I did it for the Huns when we were slaughtering each other in the trenches, so why wouldn't I do it for an Irishman?'

'Sorry,' she said meekly, sensing that however hard her life had been it simply couldn't compare with the horrors he had seen. 'And I shouldn't have hit you, I don't know why I did it.'

'Don't mind that, I've taken harder knocks. This one at least I fully deserved.'

'Will you come to the hall,' she pleaded. 'I took him some food and he won't wake up. He's dying, I'm sure of it.'

'Did you not tell Peter?'

'I can't. Jack asked me not to last night,' she cried. 'I don't know what Peter would do if I did tell him. Just now he said to me that Jack wasn't a real brother to him any more.'

'Peter wouldn't hand over his own brother no matter what he might have said.'

'Maybe not,' Nora said uncertainly, 'but this Captain Doyle fellow is watching Peter. Colonel O'Brien said so. He wouldn't suspect me or you.'

Alec didn't look convinced.

'Do you realise what you're asking me to do, Nora,' he said. 'These lads have been shooting ex-British Army men like myself.'

Nora knew from reading the newspapers that this was true. She felt her plan was crumbling on its shaky foundations. Then, to her surprise, he relented. 'Did he have a fever?'

'Yes. And he got terribly sick in the outhouse.'

In spite of the sun's warmth she shivered violently and he put his arm on her shoulder. She didn't shrink away from him.

'Now, take it easy and we'll sort out what to do.'

He considered the matter for a moment. She was amazed

at how sober he now seemed and wondered if his drunkenness wasn't sometimes just an act. After all, he'd been the same only hours before he'd fixed her up when she'd fallen in the hall. His calmness was reassuring.

'Right,' he said finally. 'I'll go and get a few bits and pieces at Brennan's Medical Hall. He's a good sort and he won't ask any questions.'

'Thanks, Alec,' she blurted out, 'I mean Mr Smithson.'

'I prefer "Alec", myself,' he smiled. 'Now, there is another problem.'

'What's that?'

'We're going to have to go to the hall pretty often in the next couple of days. So we'll need a reasonable excuse.'

This was something Nora hadn't got around to considering. She was getting more than a little weary of all the complications Jack's illness was throwing up.

'The piano,' Alec said.

'No!' she exclaimed.

'It's the only thing I can think of,' he insisted. 'You'll have to pretend you've asked me to give you lessons.'

'I can't do that,' she cried. 'It's a promise I made. That thing only ever brought me trouble.'

'If you can come up with something better before we get to the hall, it's fine with me.'

She followed him to the Medical Hall in the square and waited outside while he picked up the medicines he needed. No matter how hard she searched no other excuse occurred to her. She was left to decide between her own bitter promise and Jack's well-being. In the end, she had no choice but to go along with the deception.

Alec emerged from the shop five minutes later and gave her a questioning look.

'I'll do it,' she said, 'but I know I'll be sorry. I just know it.'

Chapter 14

'It's true,' Nora told Peter and Molly. 'I *do* want to take piano lessons again.'

'Maybe,' Alec said, 'you'd prefer to get a proper teacher.'

They had come to expect the unexpected from their niece but they were nonetheless surprised at this latest turn of events. At last Peter found he could speak, if only haltingly.

'No, Alec,' he stammered, 'it's ... it's not that at all.'

'It's wonderful!' Molly enthused. 'Nora, are you sure it's what you really want. We don't want you to be doing it only for our sakes.'

'I do miss playing,' Nora said and it was true, 'and I do want to get back to it,' she added, which wasn't at all true.

'You know, Nora,' Peter told her, 'when your mother wrote to us about you, it seems like years ago now, but she said you wouldn't want to go next nor near a piano and there was no use in forcing you, good and all as you were at it.'

Nora was sorry he'd mentioned her mother and struggled with herself to hold back an angry reply. But he went on.

'And she said when the time was right you'd realise it was something you had to do.'

'So, when will you make a start,' Molly said happily.

'No time like the present,' Alec answered for Nora and she nodded her head vigorously.

'By God,' Peter said, 'there's a woman in a hurry!'

'But you'll both freeze out there now,' Molly exclaimed.

'Oh, it's a grand day out now,' Nora said, 'and ... and I'd be afraid if I didn't do it now, I might change my mind.'

Alec and Nora began to make for the door, both suddenly struck by the same sense of urgency. Already, an hour had passed since Nora's grim discovery.

'Hold on a minute,' Peter called and she felt the hairs rise on the nape of her neck.

They both turned slowly like children caught out in some mischief or other.

'I can't have you ...' he started.

'Uncle Peter,' Nora cried desperately.

'Take it handy, girl,' he said. 'I was just going to say I can't have Alec here giving you lessons for nothing. It wouldn't be right.'

'If it wasn't for you, Peter,' Alec assured him, 'I wouldn't have a penny to my name. It's about time I paid you back.'

'We'll fix up something,' Peter insisted.

'If she gives me a hard time,' Alec laughed, 'I might put in for a few bob.'

Soon they were in the hall and when they opened the door beneath the stage she saw that Jack hadn't moved an inch since she'd left.

'He's dead, isn't he,' she whispered.

'The last thing we need is panic,' Alec said crossly as he examined Jack.

When he'd bandaged Nora, the fact that he left his tight-fitting gloves on was a mere irritation. Now, it positively annoyed her.

'Why don't you take off those stupid gloves?' she snapped. 'You can't work properly with those on you!'

Without taking his attention from Jack he muttered firmly, 'Mind your own damn business. Now go in to the house and get me a basin of hot water. Tell them I want to soak my bunions.'

'I can't say that. They wouldn't believe me.'

'Do it!'

She knew he wouldn't take no for an answer. The idea seemed ridiculous and certain to raise their suspicions. Nevertheless she went to the house and found there was method in his madness.

'Poor Alec,' Molly said, 'the feet are at him again.'

She filled a basin from the big kettle on the range and offered to carry it out.

'No, I'll do it.'

'There you go then,' Molly said, too busy to notice Nora's anxiety.

By the time she'd made her way gingerly across the yard, taking care not to spill the steaming water over her hands, Alec had managed somehow to rouse Jack from his coma. She knelt down beside the two men and watched as Alec made up a poultice from the contents of a yellow jar and a small box of white powder.

'Is he going to be all right?'

'Hasn't he the best thing short of a doctor looking after him?' Alec joked.

Jack's eyes were bloodshot and the dark circles beneath them looked like discoloured bruises. He hadn't seemed to notice Nora yet and stared almost wildly at the high ceiling of the hall.

'Jack,' she whispered.

'He hasn't said a word yet,' Alec warned. 'Best leave him be for a while. Go on over to the piano and play something.'

She felt sick and began to wonder if Jack was worth making this huge sacrifice for. At that moment she would have preferred to have taken an axe to the piano than to play it. Her hands trembled and she felt a sudden twinge of pain in her elbow.

'I can't do it,' she said. 'My elbow's at me something terrible.'

Alec turned impatiently and fixed her with an icy stare.

'You dragged me into this,' he said. 'Now, do your bit. If they don't hear some music coming out of here soon, they'll be wondering what's up.'

'I'll see to Jack,' she said foolishly, 'and you can play.'

'Stop beating around the bush. We all have to do things we don't like. Anyway, they'd know it wasn't you playing.'

'You think you're better than me,' Nora burst out, her pride hurt.

'You said it, not me.'

She stormed away furiously. As far as she was concerned, there was no doubt he was the better musician but she felt it was unkind of him to say so. It proved once again to her that he was no gentleman.

Lifting the battered lid of the piano, she sat down heavily and glared at the keys. Cracked and worn, they reminded her of the sneering, broken-toothed grin of a drunken man. She squeezed her hands into white-knuckled fists. The same vengeful anger swept through her as in that moment before she'd hit Alec.

She wanted to hit him again, and her father too, and Jack for making her break her promise and even Peter for being so much kinder to her than her father ever was. She opened out her hands and stared at her chubby fingers. How could these miserable stumps of things make anything that was beautiful or good?

The keys felt surprisingly warm under the rays of sun beaming in by the high window above her.

'I'm sorry, Mam,' she whispered aloud and banged out an uneven double arpeggio of C with both hands.

The huge sound crashed through the hall and echoed back to her.

'Hey!' Alec called. 'Are you trying to smash the thing or what?'

'Sorry.'

She remembered Mrs Teehan and imagined how she would have gasped in horror at such an abuse of her beloved instrument. The broken sound still drifted around the empty spaces of the hall.

'*Give every note a life of its own,*' she heard Mrs Teehan repeat as she had done so often. '*Let each one ring out clearly.*'

She tried once more, this time taking the painstaking care her old teacher would have expected of her.

'*Listen,*' Nora heard her voice as if she was standing beside her, '*to the clear notes winging back to you like the birds in spring.*'

Another voice came to mind. Her mother's. Young and happy, speaking the words of her poem.

> '*We walked along towards Templemore*
> *On a sunlit day in Spring*
> *And stopped awhile in Morleys wood*
> *To hear the young birds sing.*'

The clear connection between her mother's and Mrs Teehan's words lit up the darkness in her mind. It was like a nod of approval from them both, convincing her that she was doing the right thing. She began to play.

The last piece she'd learned with Mrs Teehan was an *Étude*

by Chopin. She had mastered it so well that she'd often played it without once looking up at the sheet music. In fact, she had constantly to be warned about this before the exam. To the examiners this would have been a mortal sin, even if it was played as precisely and perfectly as Nora did.

She faltered a little as she touched out the first gentle wave of notes on the left hand.

Determined to get it right she conjured up a vision of the stern-faced examiner in his fancy bow-tie, the monocle clamped in his beady eye attached by a narrow strip of red ribbon to his black velvet jacket. She told herself as she had back then that the fear would pass as soon as she plunged into the playing. And as before, the world faded away, so immersed did she become in music.

Mrs Teehan had once told her mother that this was the true measure of musical genius. The more completely you entered the spirit of the music, leaving all thoughts of anything else behind you, the greater your playing became. She had also told Mrs Canavan, as Nora sat red-faced with embarrassment in the warm music room, that never before had she seen such concentration in a girl of her age.

Now, the soft roll of notes came with such pure clarity that the very far-flung corners of the big hall rang with it. As her right hand came into play, Nora had a sensation of such power that she was driven on and on, the swell of music resounding all around her. It seemed as if time itself paused to catch its breath at her brilliance. Until and until ...

The piece ended and Nora withdrew her hands. She folded her arms around herself to hold in the heave of emotion that threatened to rip her apart. A hand touched her shoulder and she wanted to turn and bury her head in the protection of someone's arms. Even if it was Alec. But the feeling passed just as surely as the last echoes of the music.

'My God!' Alec said. 'I've never heard anything like it in my life.'

She stood up, keeping her face turned away.

'It's only a simple piece,' she snapped. 'I'm sure you could play it with your eyes closed.'

'There's no such thing as a simple piece when it's played like that,' he exclaimed. 'And at your age.'

She faced him squarely, her blushes now vanished.

'Are you calling me a child.'

'I'm calling you a musician!' he said. 'A born musician.'

'You know well you can play better than me,' she said. 'And I don't need your old plámás.'

'Nora, I'm thirty-five years old,' he said holding out his gloved left hand, 'and I can't play an arpeggio as smooth as yours. Not with this useless thing.'

'It doesn't seem so useless when you play.'

'Now you're plámásing me,' he laughed and she managed a weak smile.

From his hiding place, Jack moaned and his phlegmy cough rasped through Alec's laughter. They went quickly to his side. Alec sat him up and asked Nora to keep him steady. He began to beat him hard on the back. Nora was appalled at the violence of his blows.

'Has to be done, Nora,' Alec gasped, short of breath and hit Jack again between the shoulders. Suddenly, Jack's head shot forward and she lost her grip on his arm. An enormous lump of phlegm burst from his mouth and Nora lurched away holding her hand to her lips.

'Now we're in business,' Alec said with a huge sigh of relief. 'We'll get some of that warm water into him now and a few drops of this.'

He filled the cup Nora had brought out earlier and tipped some of the yellow medicine into it. Jack gagged on the water at first but eventually Alec succeeded in making him swallow it. He lowered Jack to the ground and wrapped him in the moth-eaten curtain.

'He'll soon be on the mend,' Alec told her. 'It's just a matter of keeping a close eye on him and I'm afraid that means another music lesson this evening.'

'Oh, no!' she sighed unconvincingly. 'Do we really have to?'

'I'll have to see him in a few hours,' he said. 'This is the crucial time.'

Jack had drifted back into a troubled sleep and his tortured face seemed to cry out for help. It occurred to her that there were many others in these awful days who cried out for help too. All too often it was because of the actions of men like Jack.

'Is he worth doing all this for?' Nora asked.

'The man is ill, that's all that matters for now,' Alec retorted. 'And if he's Peter's brother I can't believe he's as bad as they make out.'

Chapter 15

Nora sat apprehensively between Molly and Peter at the kitchen table. She wondered if she was stretching her luck too far by asking to go to the hall so soon again. Her question hung in the air while they considered it.

'Surely, one lesson is enough for today,' Peter said, 'with that elbow and all. It can't be good for it.'

'But there's so much I have to catch up with,' Nora pleaded.

'Peter is only thinking of your own good,' Molly said.

It was the wrong time to throw a tantrum but she thought of something that might convince them.

'I want to do it for my Mam's sake!' she cried, but rather guiltily.

There was nothing Peter could do but give in to her.

'Well, maybe for half an hour,' he said, 'but that's all, mind.'

Now that the tension had disappeared Nora talked enthusiastically about how she had begun so awkwardly and how the whole Chopin piece had come back to her like it was only yesterday she'd learned it.

'Chopin, no less,' Peter whistled. 'Would he be one of the Chopins from Two Mile Borris, I wonder?'

'Don't be silly,' Nora grinned, 'he was from Poland and Mrs Teehan said they called him "The Poet of the Piano".'

At the mention of Mrs Teehan's name, Peter looked questioningly at Molly.

'Maybe you should tell her now,' he said mysteriously.

Nora became anxious again. She felt she couldn't bear the strain of bad news at a time like this, there was already so much to worry about.

'We got a letter from Mrs Teehan two weeks ago and ...' Molly began.

'Why would she be writing to you?' Nora wondered aloud.

'She wanted to let us know how important it was for us to encourage you to play the piano again.'

'We thought it best to let it lie for a while,' Peter added, 'like your mother said.'

'You might write to Mrs Teehan sometime,' Molly suggested.

Nora couldn't see the point of writing. The chances were they'd never meet again in any case. Writing to her now would only make both of them sad.

'Why should I?' she said too sharply.

'Do you know what she said,' Molly went on.

Nora stood up from the table. Whatever it was she didn't want to hear it. She tried to stop Molly from going on.

'I ... I forgot to bring in the basin from the hall,' she stammered.

'She said she hasn't been so lonely since her poor husband died.'

'It's not my fault!' Nora shouted. 'I'm lonely too and no-one writes to me.'

Molly put her hand on her mouth and shook her head.

'I'm sorry, I should never have mentioned it.'

'No, you shouldn't,' Nora said bitterly.

'Here now, Nora,' Peter objected. 'There's no need to talk like that to your aunt.'

'Leave me alone, the pair of you!' she cried and ran from the kitchen and upstairs to the safe haven of her room. She paced angrily around refusing to give in to the tiredness that was coming over her.

The gentle tapping on the door had gone on for a good two minutes before she called out impatiently.

'Who is it?'

'It's Alec. Can I come in?'

'I suppose,' she answered wearily.

Alec came and stood by the window.

'Listen,' he said. 'I'll sneak over to the hall myself later on. You need to rest.'

'I'm going,' she snapped. 'There's enough people telling me what's good for me without you starting.'

'Fine,' he said patiently. 'Fine.'

In spite of the determination in her voice, Nora found it difficult to move herself. She knew that Alec was right and rest was what she really needed but she was afraid that if she did lie down she would start thinking and feeling sorry for herself again.

'I heard about what happened below,' Alec told her.

''Course they'd have to tell you!'

'They're concerned about you, Nora, that's all,' he said. 'It's hard on them when they've never had a family of their own. They feel that maybe they're not able to handle you properly.'

Nora turned cold.

'I know what it is,' she said. 'They want to get rid of me.'

'You know that isn't true. They'd do anything to make you happy.'

'You can tell them I'll be out of here as soon as I get the chance.'

'And where will you go?' he smiled annoyingly.

'Don't you dare laugh at me,' she cried. 'I'll go back to Dublin and ... find a place ... somewhere.'

Even as she said these words she saw the futility of them. There was no place for her to go. She had no choice but to stay.

'I know how you feel,' Alec said, sitting down at the window-sill. 'We're both on our own and it doesn't matter how nice people are to us, we still feel like we're locked out from the world we want to be in.'

'But you're a man,' she said impatiently, 'you can go anywhere you want to. You're not trapped like I am.'

Alec gazed out of the window and she saw the outline of his disappointed face.

'I've already been out in that big world,' he said, 'and there's nowhere I want to go back to.'

Then he turned to her with a look of great urgency and went on.

'Nora, your whole future is ahead of you and Peter and Molly are there to give you every chance. Don't let it slip away like I did.'

'I don't need anybody's charity.'

'Everyone needs to be helped,' he told her. 'Look at Jack out there. It's easy to see he's sick because his body is shaking with fever but we're all sick in our hearts sometimes. If no-one offers to help or if we refuse the help that's offered, the sickness spreads into our very souls and we never get well, never find contentment.'

He stopped abruptly and got to his feet.

'We have work to do!' he said firmly and Nora followed him down the narrow stairs and out into the pale evening light. Every last sprinkling of snow was now gone, even in those corners where the sun hadn't reached. The yard was dull and ordinary again. In fact, it was positively gloomy.

Their spirits lifted when they found Jack eating the bread and corned beef Nora had brought earlier.

'It didn't take you long to get the appetite back,' Alec laughed.

'I haven't eaten for a week,' Jack said. 'I thought I'd never eat again.'

'Don't get any ideas about taking off now,' Alec insisted. 'You need to build yourself up for a couple of days.'

'I don't know. Maybe tomorrow?'

'Forget it,' Alec said, 'you'd be on the flat of your back in no time.'

'You're right, I suppose. And listen, I want to thank the two of you for what you've done.'

'It's Nora you want to thank. She's one tough lady when it comes to twisting arms, I can tell you!'

Nora wasn't pleased with this back-handed compliment and it showed.

'See what I mean?' Alec cried. 'Now, Nora, one box in the ear is enough for one day. Go over there and play something before you're tempted to belt me again.'

The two men grinned widely at her obvious discomfort. She went away in a huff and threw back the piano lid roughly. Being made fun of in front of Jack was bad enough. The fact that he hadn't even tried to defend her was worse.

'What'll I play?' she shouted back to Alec. 'I don't know what to play.'

'There's a few pages of sheet music in the piano stool. Just lift the seat.'

She searched through the reams of yellowed paper for some familiar piece but found none. The melody that Alec played so often and which had come, in a way, to haunt her, was probably here. However, she wasn't in the mood to give Alec the satisfaction of hearing her struggle with it. He would, perhaps, offer to teach it to her and after this latest insult that was the last thing she wanted.

Finally, she decided on a waltz called 'Evening Shades'. It was a simple enough piece and it didn't take her long to work it out. If all of the pieces were as easy for her to learn as this one, surely, she thought, she could play for the pictures just as well as Alec did.

The very notion set her hands trembling and her fingers slipped on to wrong notes, in spite of herself. She made herself feel better by convincing herself that this wasn't real music. Mrs Teehan had told her that one day she would be a concert pianist and she had always imagined hushed audiences of well-dressed ladies and gentlemen, listening, enraptured by her virtuoso playing and clapping politely as she bowed to their genteel acclaim.

The reality of the ragged crowd in the Stella Cinema was so utterly different that she was amazed at herself for imagining, for one moment, that she'd want to perform for them. She knew it wasn't what Alec had planned for himself either.

'I'll play for a bit,' he called and her left hand slipped on to a jumble of clashing notes, 'Jack wants a few words with you.'

'But it's getting late,' she said, suddenly overcome by shyness. She wanted to talk to Jack but didn't really know what she might say to him.

'Go on,' Alec said, 'he won't eat you.'

She went reluctantly to where Jack lay and before he could speak, blurted out.

'I have to go back.'

His sky-blue eyes were already less bloodshot and try as she might she couldn't help looking into them.

'I just wanted to know how you were getting on since you came down from Dublin,' he smiled. 'It must be a great change from Inchicore.'

'There's nothing wrong with Inchicore.'

''Course not,' Jack said, 'they're treating you well, are they?'

'I suppose,' she murmured.

'You don't sound too sure.'

'I'm only in the way,' Nora said.

'I can't believe that, Nora.'

'Well, it's true,' Nora's voice shook. 'I hate them.'

'That's a desperate thing to say.'

'You're one to talk! You hate your own brother.'

'I do not indeed!'

'You don't trust him,' she said angrily. 'If you did, you'd ask him to help you and not go dragging us into all this.'

'I don't want to get himself or Molly into trouble,' he said uncomfortably.

'But you don't mind getting us into it.'

'I know. I shouldn't have asked you. It's not right.'

They both sat quietly as Alec played the same piece Nora had just learned. She thought he made it sound so much better than she had and this only added to her anger and frustration.

'Why don't you talk to Colonel O'Brien? He wants to try and settle things — or don't you trust him either?'

'You couldn't find a more honourable man in Ireland,' Jack said.

'He says they're offering an amnesty,' Nora told him. 'He told Peter he wants to meet you about it.'

Jack looked away into the dark, musty spaces beneath the stage.

'It's not that simple,' he said, at last. 'I could talk to O'Brien in the morning but unless I can get my men to agree with me, it would be a waste of time. And besides we have our own Colonels and most of them wouldn't have it. They're determined to keep the fight going, no matter what.'

'What about you?'

'I don't know,' he said. 'An amnesty is another word for surrender and they won't have it, my lads. I know the numbers are against us but things have happened that can't be forgotten. I suppose it's the same on both sides. The longer it goes on, the more revenge comes into it. Just fighting to get them back for what they've done to us.'

'But that can't be right,' Nora said despairingly. 'That way it'll never end.'

'The thing is,' Jack said, fixing his hypnotic eyes on her, 'as long as I can stay in charge of my own men I can keep things under control in these parts. We'll blow up a few bridges and knock some trees across the roads but there'll be no killing and no thieving. If I give up now there's others only too willing to take over and things would go from bad to worse.'

'Why can't you just leave people in peace?' she said, storming away angrily.

Alec followed her out of the hall and asked her what was wrong.

'There's nothing wrong,' she shouted. 'Only that ungrateful murderer wants to keep fighting when he knows they can't win.'

'Calm down, Nora,' Alec pleaded. 'They'll hear you inside.'

'Get out of my way, you drunken old fool,' she said and left him standing in the yard, scratching his head in wonder and amusement at her outburst.

If she hadn't been equally angry with Molly and Peter that evening as she was with Jack she might have told them the whole story, there and then. Instead, she went directly to her room and when Molly came to the door she turned to the wall and ignored her call.

Jack, she decided, was no better than her father in his ingratitude for her efforts. She wondered if there was anyone in the world worth doing anything for now that her mother was gone. Even her brothers hadn't bothered to write to her, she thought, and immediately felt foolish. After all they were only children. The only person she could think kindly of was Rosie Tobin, her good neighbour in Inchicore and she longed to have her there to tell her what to do.

As the dark hours passed she found her anger settling finally on Mrs Teehan. Whey couldn't she have written to Nora instead of to her aunt and uncle? If she really cared she would surely have done so.

In the end she promised herself that she'd see Jack through his illness and then wash her hands of him altogether. When he was gone she would continue the new life she had been forced to live as if she had never met him.

As her eyes closed she was able to believe that it was all very simple. A few days and this little crisis would be over. Over and done with.

Chapter 16

During the following days, a sense of calm descended on Nora. In spite of all the coming and going at the hall and constant practising of pieces she felt were almost beneath her dignity and the continuing effort of pretence with her aunt and uncle, this welcome feeling stayed with her.

It helped her to behave more decently towards Peter and Molly and even Alec. Above all, it helped her to put aside her exasperation with Jack and come as close to friendliness as it was possible to do, in the circumstances. If it was the calm before a raging storm she saw no dark clouds on the horizon.

News that might have been bad news before, left her untroubled. When Molly told her that the school was to open in three weeks, it didn't seem half the calamity it might have earlier.

In the *Tipperary Star* she read the terms of the amnesty and was unmoved by the threat it contained beneath its words of conciliation. It seemed like the Irregulars were being given their last chance. After this, they would get little mercy if caught. She knew, nonetheless, that it would be pointless showing it to Jack.

Then Jimmer arrived with the familiar envelope from her father on Friday and though she noticed that Molly wasn't as welcoming as usual she thought nothing of it. As he sat and drank his tea in the kitchen he said something that should have left her broken-hearted.

'The boys are gone to America. Jim is in bits above.'

'I'm sorry I had to bring this news, Nora,' Jimmer said.

'It's for the best,' Nora answered flatly.

Molly made some excuses about being busy and hurried Jimmer away to the front door. When she returned Nora was holding the envelope in her hand. She didn't want to talk about what had just been said but she wanted to see what her father had to say about it. In truth, she merely wanted to confirm for herself her certainty that he missed them more than he ever missed her.

'Will I open this for you?' she asked and stood open-mouthed as Molly snatched it from her hand.

'Don't!' Molly said. 'It's ... it's probably better you don't see what's in it.'

'It's only money, isn't it?'

'Yes, but ... there's a letter too and it's bound to be, I don't know, sad. You don't really want to see that.'

'I suppose not,' Nora said, thinking bitterly that she didn't need Molly to protect her from her father's cold-heartedness.

She turned her mind to the more urgent concerns of the moment. Where would she get the next plate of food for Jack? How long more would it take for him to get well enough to leave? Had any of the neighbours noticed the extra activity at the hall and perhaps passed the word on to Captain Doyle?

Already, they had had one lucky break. There was to be no show this Friday because a concert was to be held else-

where in town that night. That was one less worry. All the
same, Jack hadn't improved quite as quickly as Alec had
expected and she feared that come next Friday the same
problem would face them.

Yet, in a real way, all these worries were welcome ones,
particularly now that the break-up of her family was complete. They kept her occupied but were not the kind that
induced terrible panic. They were simply small concerns that
would resolve themselves.

'Are you all right?' Molly asked. 'You seem very quiet in
yourself.'

'I'm grand,' was all Nora would say.

'You shouldn't think your father puts more heed in losing
the boys than in losing you,' Molly said, amazed at how
unconcerned Nora seemed to be.

Nora sipped her tea and nibbled her bread. She would let
nothing that anybody said or did, touch her. She felt her heart
was a small animal in hibernation from the cold of the world.

Alec too was surprised at her new-found serenity. Even
more surprising was the fact that she actually began to show
a real interest and concern for him. He couldn't make sense
of this sudden change.

'You know something,' she told him, 'you could make a
really good doctor if you put your mind to it.'

As usual, he raised his gloved hand with its stiff finger.

'With this hand?' he laughed but she was undaunted.

'That's only an excuse. Didn't you fix up Jack?'

'He's not right yet.'

'Well, he will be,' she said firmly. 'You're giving me bad
example with your lame excuses, don't you know that?'

'But ... but ...'

'But, but, but,' she mimicked. 'What are you — an old goat
or what?'

Over at the hall her mood swung so quickly from quiet calm to high spirits and back again that the two men often exchanged questioning glances. Even these she didn't notice.

Most of the time she and Jack talked about their own pasts. She told him about her life in Dublin, the good times and the bad times. The strange thing was that as she spoke it was if all these things had happened to someone else whose story she was simply making up or had heard second-hand. Yet there was nothing second-hand about the awful aching feeling deep inside her that came with every mention of her mother.

He listened, shaking his head in disbelief at her father's harshness and her mother's hard life with him.

'Poor Annie,' he would repeat again and again.

'Did you know her very well?' Nora asked once, letting her curiosity get the better of her.

'She was the best-looking girl in town. We all knew her,' he said but added quietly, 'Well, we all thought we knew her.'

'What do you mean?'

'Ah, nobody knows what goes on in a woman's head,' he said, laughing off his discomfort.

'At least, their heads aren't empty like men's heads!' Nora retorted.

At times like these he seemed incapable of any wrongdoing. He praised her courage in enduring her father's wrath but Nora saw nothing brave in what she had done. It had simply been a matter of making the best of a bad situation for the sake of her mother and brothers. In fact, in her heart, she felt she was a coward for never really standing up to her father.

His story seemed infinitely more exciting. He described how he and Peter and some others from the town, like Colonel O'Brien had fought against Black 'n' Tans in the struggle for independence. He told her how one of his best friends was chased and shot by them out in the countryside. How the Tans threw the dead man's body into the back of a truck with his legs hanging out all the way into town and stopped outside his mother's house, shouting abuse at her and laughing at her anguished cries.

Then there was his life on the run: trying to get food and shelter in the hills and admitting to robbing food supplies that were carried from town to town. He insisted they only took what they needed for themselves but guessed there were others who took more.

Three years he had spent now without a home. He told her that fewer and fewer of his old friends welcomed him when he looked for a hiding place for the night. It was hard to blame them, he agreed, there were such terrible tales of barbarity on the Irregular side these days.

However, he never went any further than this admission. When their conversation drifted to things like this he always returned quickly to safer ground lest they should begin to argue.

As the days passed there seemed to be less and less time to work on the piano, which didn't bother Nora. Yet, during this time she mastered six pieces from Alec's bundle and actually came to enjoy the challenge she set herself of learning each one more quickly than the one before.

Every morning she woke to the bright prospect of meeting Jack again and rediscovering something of her joy in the uncomplicated music. Always, however, there was the certainty that Jack had his dark secrets, perhaps even blood on his hands, and this held her back from true friendship. They could laugh and talk but that distance would always remain between them.

In any case, he would soon be gone and his life was such

a dangerous one that it could end, at any time, in violent death. These thoughts though constantly in her mind never took away from the warm wash of feeling that daylight brought with it.

She was as well prepared as she could be, then, for the disappointment that came when this happy interlude began to reach its end.

The first hint of change came at the breakfast table one dark rain-filled morning. The kitchen was uncomfortably quiet as she entered. She guessed that something unpleasant lay behind Molly and Peter's sudden attempts at cheerfulness. She waited impatiently to hear the inevitable bad news. By the time she had finished her tea and bread there was still no clue as to what was up.

'Something's wrong,' she said.

Peter's face took on a pained expression as he tried to speak. He shook his head and got up from the table. He stared forlornly at the space above their heads and left the kitchen without a word.

Nora's doubts about Jack flooded back. He may not have been the actual robber but might he not have been lying about the fact that no-one else knew where he was? There was nothing stopping him from giving orders.

'It's gone beyond the beyonds,' Molly said in despair. 'They broke into the Parish Priest's house and fired a shot over his head. Have they lost all sense of decency?'

'The priest's house!' Nora repeated in astonishment.

'Can you imagine, Nora, they stole money from the collection boxes, the poor people's money?'

'I'm going out to practice,' Nora said in a daze of confusion.

'Nora, we need you in the shop today,' Molly said. 'Peter is in no fit state for work, he's so upset.'

Nora realised rather guiltily that she'd done little or nothing around the house and shop these last few days. She wondered if this wasn't a thinly-disguised hint. Nevertheless, she did as she was asked as cheerfully as she could.

The hours dragged by slowly and when, at last, she got a chance to go to the hall, her feelings for Jack had run cold. She strode resolutely across the yard and lane and into the hall, brushing off his usual warm greeting.

'Where are you hiding the money?'

'You know I couldn't have done that robbery last week,' he said. 'I was a stretcher case, for God's sake!'

'Not last night, you weren't.'

'What are you talking about, girl?'

Still hoping he was innocent of this latest outrage, at least, she kept up her attack.

'You or one of your cronies broke into the priest's house last night.'

He rubbed his chin with a firm hand. Lost in thought, he ignored her questioning gaze.

'What have you to say for yourself?' she raged.

'Look, Nora, this is as much a shock to me as it is to you. I don't know what to think.'

'So, you didn't do it,' she sneered. 'And I suppose you didn't do anything else either. Aren't you a pure saint!'

His eyes narrowed and the soft, clear blue in them was suddenly dark and threatening. She took fright at the change in him and stepped back.

'I've done things,' he began, 'things no man should have to do. But I swear to you, I had no part in any of these robberies. None!'

'What kind of things?' she muttered fearfully.

'I've killed, Nora,' he said so quietly she could just about hear. 'Killed my enemies and men who were once my friends.

It's a war, dammit, it was me or them.'

He seemed to be pleading with her to understand. She felt queasy, her head dizzied by his words.

'I never shot a man who didn't have a gun in his hand,' he went on.

She wanted to run away from this place, from this man who had killed other men, left grieving families behind. Her legs were too weak to carry her. His face had lost its healthiness and he now looked worse than on the night she had found him. Once, she had regarded herself as an outcast much like him. Now she saw that he was more lost than she could ever become.

'Even if I live to see an end to this war,' he said, 'I'll never be the same again. I'll never have a minute's peace or rest.'

Nora sank to her knees. She felt the whole weight of his guilt and misery pressing on her.

'Sometimes,' he told her, 'I wish I could die in the fight. That way, I won't have to live with myself when it's over.'

'You shouldn't say things like that,' Nora whispered, amazed at herself for having even an ounce of sympathy left for him. 'Aunt Molly says you're a good man. So does Colonel O'Brien.'

She was trying to convince herself as much as Jack.

'Maybe I was once,' he said but if he had any more to add it was lost beneath Alec's muted call from the hall door.

'Nora, is he still here?'

'I'm here,' Jack answered.

'Thank God for that,' Alec said with relief. 'You heard about last night, Jack?'

'I did,' Jack replied grimly. 'Alec, will you do one more thing for me. If you can't, I'll understand.

'I suppose,' Alec agreed nervously.

'I have to make my way out of here but I'll need some help.

I want you, if you think you can, to get a message to someone.'

'Ah, Jack, you can't be serious.'

'It just means calling to a house and leaving word there.'

Nora gave Alec a pleading look.

'Well,' Alec said finally, 'I was born a fool, so I'll always be one. Where's the house?'

'Do you know Maguires out in Ballyhack?'

'Tim Maguire?'

'That's it,' Jack said, 'All you have to do is tell them where I am. They'll do the rest.'

'Does this mean you'll be leaving tomorrow?' Nora wondered aloud.

'I'd go tonight if I could,' Jack told her. 'And I'll tell you one thing — if any of my lads are caught up in this thieving, I'll ...'

'Kill them!' Nora exclaimed in her shock.

'No, no ... I'll just make sure it never happens again. And Nora.'

'Yes,' she said sharply.

'Not a word to Peter. Not a word.'

'I'm making no more promises to you or anybody else.'

'I'll leave it up to yourself, then.'

'Go to hell,' she spat out bitterly.

'I suppose I will,' he said. 'I suppose I will.'

Before long Alec was on his way to Ballyhack and Nora was back in the house. She spent the rest of the day looking for jobs to do. In her mind she swung from making excuses for Jack's killing of other men to disgust and sheer terror at the thought of such violence.

She found herself avoiding Peter at every turn. Soon, it might be too late. His despairing words haunted her all day. 'I wish I could die in the fight.'

In the end, she couldn't go against Jack's wishes and kept

a reluctant silence. After all, he would be gone elsewhere and even if he did die, she would not be the cause of it.

That night when her head touched the pillow she didn't so much fall asleep as tumble headlong into a dark chasm that was empty of all hope and contentment.

Just after two in the morning she was disturbed by an infernal racket. Still half-asleep she dragged herself up and peered out of the back window.

The Parnell Hall was surrounded by dozens of Free State soldiers! At the very moment she looked out, a lamp was raised to a small weasel-like face. She had never seen him before but something told her it was Captain Doyle.

He stood at the entrance with a pistol in his hand. She opened her window slightly and heard his hoarse, sneering yell.

'Come out, Delaney! Or you're a dead man.'

Chapter 17

Grabbing a coat from her mother's wardrobe, Nora raced downstairs. The night air was filled with shouted orders and the stamp of heavy boots. Above the noise, Captain Doyle's voice echoed loudly.

'Give yourself up and there'll be no shooting.'

She could hear Peter somewhere up ahead.

'I'm warning you, Doyle, if you shoot him ...' he yelled.

'You'll do what?' Doyle taunted him.

Nora felt an arm reach over her shoulder and squirmed away from it.

'It's all right, Nora,' Molly said. 'It's only me.'

'What will they do to him, Molly?' Nora asked, no longer sure that it mattered in the least to her.

'Jack wouldn't be fool enough to hide in there,' Molly assured her.

'But if he had to,' Nora said, in spite of herself. 'If he was sick or something.'

Nora realised she'd said too much as Molly turned her

around face to face. She was about to speak when a loud crash swept their attention away to the door of the hall. They spun around and saw Captain Doyle's boot smashing it open. Shots rang out all around them and Nora screamed, holding Molly tightly.

A young soldier ran over to where they stood.

'For God's sake, Mrs Delaney, will you get back in the house and take the girl with you.'

'I will not indeed. Anyway, you know as well as I do, he's not in there.'

'He is, Missus,' the soldier said, 'we got a tip-off. He's hiding under the stage.'

Nora was frozen to the spot. Only one other person could have known where Jack was. It seemed clear that Alec had gone directly to Captain Doyle instead of to the Maguires out in Ballyhack. She felt so bitterly towards him that she supposed he'd done it for drinking money. For one terrible moment she understood how you could hate someone enough to kill them.

Silence fell over the yard and hall. Molly and Nora edged closer to the door where two armed soldiers stood at each side aiming their rifles at the tense, dark, stillness inside. Captain Doyle was there too, waiting impatiently for Jack to show some sign of surrender.

'Delaney,' he yelled. 'We'll burn you out of it if we have to.'

There was no sound from the cavernous dark. Captain Doyle called a group of soldiers around him. Nora couldn't make out what he was saying but it was obvious they were preparing an attack. He pointed to the two long windows above the door and the others helped two men to climb on to the wide ledges there. An ear-splitting crash followed as they both broke in panes of glass and eased the barrels of their rifles inside.

The two soldiers at the door lit oil lamps and carefully placed them just inside, out of sight. An eerie light ascended like a grey stain over the chairs and benches. From where they stood, Nora and Molly could see the faint outline of the stage. Nora couldn't keep her eyes from the small door inside which she knew, better than anyone, Jack lay. She wondered whether he wasn't happy that now he would have his chance 'to die in the fight'.

Now, Captain Doyle stood behind five or six soldiers with his hand-gun at the ready. She heard him count quietly. One: the men crouched in readiness. Two: Captain Doyle raised his left arm. Three: with boots thundering across the timber floor and guns blazing they charged through the door, diving for cover behind chairs and whatever else came to hand. Molly gasped and tried to cover Nora's face but she wanted to see, no matter how awful it might be, she wanted to see everything.

Again the shooting stopped and Nora could see, a little more clearly now, the small door. It was riddled with bullet holes. Surely Jack couldn't possibly have survived this assault?

The soldiers inside began to crawl towards their target until they suddenly stopped and lay still on the floor like so many fallen statues. A muffled voice had called from beneath the stage. Nora took a step forward but Molly held her back.

The voice came again and she heard a whisper pass along from one soldier to the next. One of the men crouching at the doorway called to Captain Doyle who had retreated outside when the firing began.

'He's coming out.'

'Tell the lads to fire as soon as they catch sight of him.'

'But if he's not armed?' the soldier asked.

'Shoot him anyway,' Doyle grunted. 'He'd do the same to you.'

Molly left Nora's side and ran to the sly-faced Captain. She grabbed his arm.

'You can't do that,' she pleaded. 'The man is surrendering.'

He pushed her away and raised his pistol towards her. Out of the gloom, Peter stepped between them. He caught Captain Doyle's wrist in a vice-like grip. Doyle's face was twisted with hatred and fear.

'I'll have you shot,' he stammered. 'You and your murdering brother.'

'If you ever raise your hand to my wife again, I'll make dog-meat of you.'

'I'm a Captain in the Free State Army, you can't talk to me like that.'

'You're nothing but a tramp, Doyle!' Peter said and then the cold barrel of a gun touched his temple.

'Let him go,' the soldier said.

Nora could see the man wasn't happy about having to threaten Peter like this.

'Take that gun from my head, John,' Peter said quietly, 'and I'll let this rat out of its trap.'

The soldier lowered his gun and Peter released the Captain.

'I'm going to finish off your brother now, Delaney,' Doyle leered. 'And one of these days I'll have you too!'

Peter made a move towards him but the soldier held him.

'Forget it, Peter,' he said, as the Captain strode away. 'He's not worth it. If Jack is unarmed there'll be no shots fired.'

Peter turned away and raised his head in anguish to the grey-black sky that was empty of stars. Nora peered once more at the bullet-riddled door. It began to open slowly, inch by inch.

'Put your two hands out where we can see them!' Doyle ordered.

A low mutter came from behind the opening door. Again, Nora could make no sense of it. Captain Doyle, standing in the doorway of the hall obviously heard what was said.

'Course we won't shoot you,' he shouted. 'Just get those hands out!'

The fingers of one hand emerged to grip the side of the door. They were strangely dark in the faint light like those of a coalminer clambering from a dusty pit. The other hand slowly crawled like a huge spider into view. Nora's heart skipped a beat as Captain Doyle aimed his pistol.

At that very moment, the soldier called John, crossed between Doyle and the small door.

'Get out of the way!' the Captain bellowed but the soldier had by now reached the door and kicked it open.

He reached inside and dragged the prisoner out where they could see him. Nora couldn't bear to look in their direction but noticed at once the dumbfounded expression on Captain Doyle's face. Slowly her eyes left his and followed to where they stared until she saw the object of his confusion hunched below the soldier's rifle. It was Alec.

She had never been so glad to see him. Even as she smiled widely with relief she chided herself for jumping so quickly to conclusions about him.

Meanwhile, Captain Doyle's face had turned a strange bluish-purple and a large snake-like vein throbbed along the length of his outstretched neck. The gun in his hand shook uncontrollably. He ran like a man possessed towards Alec and aimed his boot at the crumpled body. Peter tried to break through the group of soldiers guarding the hall door but they stood firm. Alec took the blow on his shoulder and rolled away.

'Where's Jack Delaney?' Captain Doyle roared.

Alec lifted his head.

'I know nothing about him,' he muttered.

Captain Doyle stepped forward but the soldier again got himself between them.

'Maybe he's still in there,' he said, pointing under the stage.

'Stand back!' Doyle ordered.

He lowered his gun to the open door and fired off three shots and with each one Nora expected to hear a scream of pain. There was no sound but the echo of the shots. He threw his gun to the ground and picked up Alec roughly.

'Where is he gone?' he barked.

'I told you,' Alec said, 'I don't know the first thing about him.'

'We *know* he was here.'

'Well, I haven't seen him and I'm here since the pub closed.'

Captain Doyle threw him on the ground and stepped away. As he stooped to get his gun, Alec spoke up.

'I know you,' he said calmly. 'You're from Mullingar, aren't you?'

The Captain eyed him suspiciously, not knowing what to expect next.

'What's it to you where I'm from?'

'My mother is from Mullingar. We used to go there to visit her people in the summers.'

'I'm not interested in your mother or ...'

'She's one of the Dempseys of Laun House,' Alec smiled mischievously. 'Your mother used to work there in the kitchen.'

Captain Doyle looked around sharply to see if any of his men had even the trace of a smile on their faces. They were more surprised than amused to see their feared Captain spoken down to like this.

'I didn't come here to make small talk,' he said but Alec showed no sign of relenting.

'You're one of the Fecker Doyles, aren't you?' he laughed.

A strangled cough came from the Captain's throat.

'Feck the milk out of your tea, people used to say,' Alec told his hushed audience.

Captain Doyle pointed his gun at him. His hand was still shaking now that his confusion had turned to rage.

'One more word out of you and I'll blow your head off!'

Alec raised his gloved hands in a mocking gesture.

'Just trying to be friendly,' he smiled. 'After our little misunderstanding.'

Nora was flabbergasted at Alec's foolhardy taunting of the Captain. She couldn't understand why he was taking such a risk. There was no doubt that Doyle was a ruthless man and talking to him like this was madness. She was even more surprised when the Captain shouted to his men again.

'We're wasting our time here.'

'Shouldn't we search the outhouses?' the soldier who'd just saved Alec's life called.

'He's well gone by now,' Doyle muttered and then pointing at Alec said, 'And you! A little bit of advice for you. Start saying your prayers.'

This time Alec had the sense to stay quiet. The hall emptied quickly until only Nora, her aunt and uncle and Alec were left. They looked around grim-faced at the wreckage about them. Chairs and benches toppled over; bullet holes all along the front of the stage and in the walls close by; lumps of broken plaster, split by the impact of the shots, fell loudly to the floor. Splinters of shattered glass crunched beneath their feet.

'How could they think he was here?' Peter asked in disbelief.

Nora's eyes met Alec's and they both looked away quickly as if neither one could decide whether to tell the truth or not.

'Doyle has his knife in you, Peter,' Alec offered at last. 'He was just looking for an excuse to get at you.'

'But they might have killed you, Alec,' Peter said, his eyes searching the place desperately, as if for clues. 'No point in doing anything with this mess until tomorrow.'

Nora was bursting to ask Alec where Jack was. Had he already left when the soldiers had arrived? Or was he still out there somewhere nearby?

In the kitchen, Nora saw that Alec was deathly pale. His hands shook so much he had to leave his tea untouched. He tried to smile but his lips twisted into a mad leer. He closed his eyes and frowned deeply.

'First thing in the morning,' Peter said, 'I'll go looking for Colonel O'Brien. He'll put a stop to this Doyle fellow.'

Molly wasn't convinced.

'We don't want to draw more trouble on ourselves,' she said. 'Maybe he'll leave us alone now he knows we've nothing to hide.'

'Not until he finds Jack,' Peter told her and turned to Alec. 'You'd better stay the night with us.'

'I'll fix up the spare room,' Nora volunteered, hoping this would give her a chance to talk to Alec.

She went to the linen closet and took out fresh sheets. As she was making up the bed she found herself hoping that this room would one day, when all the fighting had ended, be Jack's. They could all live in peace and have no secrets from each other and no memory of what had gone on before. It occurred to her that this very house had waited, in much the same way, for her mother to return. She remembered thinking how her mother's room had seemed like she had only left for a short while. But she had never come back and Nora wondered if her fervent hope would also be unfulfilled.

She listened to the heavy trudge of footsteps on the stairs and knew it must be Alec. As soon as he entered the room she could smell the whiskey from his breath. She didn't protest but he raised his hand defensively anyway.

'I just took the one,' he explained, 'to steady the nerves.'

'You needed it,' she said. 'Where's Jack?'

'I don't know,' he said, 'but the further away the better.'

'But what happened? How did they know he was in there?'

'God only knows,' he said, sitting down on the bed and lowering his voice he went on, 'but I have my suspicions.'

'What do you mean, suspicions?'

'See, I went out to Maguires like he asked and gave the message,' he was whispering now, 'and just as I was heading back out the lane, I saw out of the side of my eye, a figure at one of the windows. It wasn't one of the Maguires, I'm sure of that.'

A cold shiver went through him.

'I could feel those eyes burning in my back. I'm telling you I thought I'd never be out of there quick enough.'

'And you think he was the one who told Captain Doyle?'

'I don't know. Maybe the Maguires did, who can tell?'

'That fellow you saw,' she said suddenly fearful, 'he might have been one of Jack's men. Who else would have been hiding in the house?'

'Maybe so.'

'And he could be the one doing the robberies,' she cried. 'What did he look like?'

'Nora, you're jumping the gun now. Besides, I didn't see his face and to be honest, I didn't want to.'

'But if it is one of his own men, we should warn him.'

'He's gone, Nora, we can't help him any more. That was

why I kept Doyle talking, so's he'd have a headstart on them.'

It was pointless arguing any further. She knew Alec had done as much as he could. He might even have died in Jack's place if it hadn't been for the soldier, John. Now that she had time to consider Alec, she felt angry with Jack for running away and leaving him to risk his life.

'Why did he sneak off,' she asked bitterly, 'and let you take his place?'

'It wasn't his idea,' he said. 'Jack didn't want to go. In fact, he was ready to give himself up.'

'And why didn't he?'

'I told him what everyone knows. Doyle would kill him before he got near a court. Even if he got that far his chances are slim.'

'Maybe he doesn't deserve any better.'

'The man is doing his best to keep his men under control. I believe that. And I believe it won't be too long before he talks to Colonel O'Brien.'

'You could have been shot,' Nora exclaimed.

'And what loss would I be to anyone?' he said wearily.

'Don't say that,' she cried.

'Inside in that hole under the stage, it was like being in the trenches again,' he said. 'The past is always there waiting for you, isn't it, girl? Waiting to drag you down.'

'It doesn't have to be like that,' she said, surprised at her thoughts. 'It's not the past that matters, it's the way you see it.'

She didn't know where the idea sprang from but it seemed right. If you dwell on the awfulness of the past, she thought, you might as well still be living through its horrors. It was like that excruciating pain that followed her fall. Terrible as it was, it had eased with time. Now and then there was a reminder of that pain but for the most part she was able to forget the accident had ever happened. Surely, it could be the same with bad memories. You will always be hurt by them but it will be less and less so as you go on.

She wished she could explain this more clearly to Alec but at this moment he seemed barely aware of her existence. She had never seen him look so lost and broken even when he was out of his mind with drink.

'You should sleep,' she said finally.

'I don't know if I'll ever sleep again,' he muttered but he lay back and his eyes closed without a flicker.

In her own room she paced around, her feet too numb to feel the night cold. Somewhere out there, Jack was making his way back to his men not realising that, perhaps, one of them had betrayed him. If one of them had done that, what else might he do when Jack was with him again. She imagined Jack with his back turned and a gun aimed in the dark at his head. She felt helpless and fell on her bed in an agony of frustration.

Something tapped on the open window. She sat up. A pebble struck the window ledge and bounced into the room. It rolled across the floor as another stone hit the window pane. She looked out into the yard.

Down below, Jack beckoned to her from the outhouse she'd found him in the week before. She knew she would have to wait some time until the house fell silent again. Even then, she guessed, her aunt and uncle might not actually be asleep. No more than herself, how could they rest after such a night?

It was, however, a chance she would have to take. Something told her that if she didn't go to him now, she might never see him again. Not alive, in any case.

Chapter 18

With her shoes in her hand, Nora took each step of the stairs with the exaggerated care of an old woman. It was difficult to hold herself back from hurrying. Dawn would soon be breaking and Jack would have to go before some early riser spotted him. By the time she reached the door into the yard she was sure he would already have given up on her.

The door squeaked on its hinges and she hesitated for another eternity. Once outside, she slipped into her shoes and ran to the outhouse. She was about to open the door when she heard Jack whisper from the lane beyond.

'Nora! Over here!'

She found him crouched behind the end wall of the yard. He looked ill again and she thought that even the air around him, reeked of sickness.

'I'm sorry to get you out in the cold,' he said 'but I had to know if Alec was all right.'

'They nearly killed him.'

'I shouldn't have let him stay there but he wouldn't listen

to me.'

'There's something you should know, Jack,' she said, realising there was no time for accusations. 'When Alec delivered your message he saw some fellow watching him from the house and it wasn't any of the Maguires.'

Jack grew even paler.

'Did he say what he looked like?'

'No, he only got a quick look,' she said. 'Do you think it might have something to do with what happened tonight?'

'Maybe.'

'What if it was one of your own men?'

She could see by his face in the growing light, that he was thinking the same thing. It was clear too that the very thought of such a thing brought him great pain.

'I think it's time,' he said at last, 'to talk to Colonel O'Brien.'

'Uncle Peter is going to see him this morning,' Nora said excitedly. 'I could tell him you want to meet the Colonel.'

'No! Keep Peter out of this,' Jack said sharply. 'We have our own way of arranging these things.'

'But ...'

'There is something you can do,' he said. 'I wouldn't ask only, to tell you the truth, I'm not sure who I can trust at this minute.'

'I'll do anything.'

'There's a hardware shop in the Square. Foleys. Go there and ask for Vincent Ryan. Have you got that?'

'Foleys. Vincent Ryan. Yes and then?'

'Tell him to bring the Red Setter to the turnpike tomorrow evening.'

He stood up stiffly as if every movement of his tired body required a huge effort.

'It's getting light,' he said with a smile. 'I'll have to make tracks.'

'Will there be peace now?' she asked.

'We'll sort out these robberies first, Nora, then we'll talk about the rest.'

'Where are you going?'

'We have a safe house not too far away. You wouldn't find better in a jungle!'

'But if that fellow tries to ...'

'Nora,' he said. 'Alec probably just imagined he saw someone at Maguires and even if he did, I'll let you in on a little secret.'

She looked at him suspiciously.

'Inside this safe house I have my own hiding-place and no-one else knows about it.' he whispered.

'I don't understand.'

'You know those big open fireplaces in country cottages? Big as a double door they are.'

'I think so,' she said doubtfully.

'Well, in this house we have in the woods, there's a secret door tucked in the side of the fireplace where it can't be seen. Inside, there's a tiny space, so small that if two people were in there they'd have to stand up and they'd still be touching.'

The idea sounded so preposterous to Nora that she felt he was inventing it just to reassure her.

'I'm not a child, you know,' she snapped. 'You don't have to make up fairy stories to make me feel better.'

'But, it's true,' he laughed, and stopped suddenly as if he felt there was no more time for laughter.

'Before I go, I want to thank you again,' he said. 'I hope I can pay you back some day for saving my life.'

'Alec did that.'

'Alec too. But if it wasn't for you he wouldn't have.'

She felt uncomfortably hot in spite of the damp chill.

'The trouble with this damned business of fighting for a

cause is that you drag other people into it with you. I'm finished with doing that. What I'm asking you to do now is the last thing I'll ask of anyone. I promise you that.'

'I'll go to Foleys,' she said. 'Don't worry.'

In spite of the risks she had taken to help him and the confession he had made to her about killing other men she couldn't bear to see him go. She had become convinced that what Molly and the Colonel and even Alec had said about him was true. He was a decent man caught up in an impossible situation, fighting not simply for the sake of fighting but for a cause he believed in.

On the other side were equally decent men like Colonel O'Brien and they just happened to believe in an opposite point of view. But there were evil men on both sides too and they would never want peace.

Now that Jack was to meet Colonel O'Brien things might begin to change. Not everywhere at once, of course, not in every part of every county. But perhaps here, in this small town in Tipperary, the light of peace might begin to glow if two honourable men could be reasonable with one another. This hope made the pain of parting a little easier for Nora.

Jack shook her hand and as the dawn traced the grim outline of the hall behind them, he walked away and with a last wave turned the corner and was gone. So preoccupied with her thoughts was she that as she opened the door of the house she completely forgot about its habit of squeaking loudly.

The noise was loud enough to wake the heaviest of sleepers. She heard a call from upstairs and stood unable to move as someone came heavily down the steps. She hoped it was Alec but even if it was him the others would be sure to follow. There would be questions and suspicions and at this moment she didn't feel able to deal with that. There was nothing she could do but close her eyes tightly as if this would make all of them go away.

'What on earth are you up to, Nora?'

It was Peter's voice. She couldn't bring herself to open her eyes and face him.

'Don't shout at her,' Molly whispered quietly. 'She's sleep-walking.'

It was a perfect excuse and Nora made the best of it. She walked slowly forward towards them, muttering to herself as she went.

'I'll take her up,' Molly said and Nora felt her arms on her shoulders, guiding her from step to step.

She heard Peter and Alec talking below.

'The poor misfortunate thing,' Peter said. 'She's known nothing only trouble all her life and God knows it's no better down here for her. Sometimes I wonder if she wouldn't be safer up in Dublin.'

'She had no life up there, Peter,' Alec consoled him, 'and this business won't last forever.'

'I don't know, Alec. Things will never be the same.'

They continued to talk but by now Molly had got Nora to her bed. She could feel her aunt's trembling fingers touch her forehead and guessed that this woman's kindly face was lined with worry. She was tempted to open her eyes and reassure her and to say that she was grateful for her care and concern. What kept her eyes closed was no longer the pretence but rather a terrible feeling of shame.

How easily lies and deceit came to her now. There always seemed to be a way to avoid the truth and she wondered if she would ever be capable of honesty again. And yet all the lies and excuses had been invented for what she believed were the right reasons — to help Jack and to protect him. It seemed to Nora that, in a real way, the guilt she felt must be very like the guilt that haunted Jack. He had killed for a cause he believed in, done the wrong thing for what he was convinced was the right reason.

How easily too she had come to accept that he had killed and continued to help him. Would it not have been different, she thought, if what Jack vaguely called 'other men', had been people she had known. Peter or Alec or Colonel O'Brien, for instance.

The truth was that these 'other men' had families too, young wives, perhaps even children. The very thought sickened her but she was consoled by the fact that Jack was making some attempt to change things.

There was no point in trying to sleep and she waited with growing apprehension to play her part in Jack's plan.

She was needed in the shop all morning. Peter had got a lift in a delivery truck to Roscrea, where he'd heard Colonel O'Brien had gone the previous day.

'Are you sure it's a good idea?' Molly had asked again before he left.

'If a man can't be left alone in peace with his family,' he said, 'he has to do something about it.'

At the kitchen door he turned to them and added, 'It's fellows like Doyle who drive people into taking sides even when they don't want to.'

Late in the afternoon when Nora was beginning to despair of ever getting to Foley's shop in the Square, Molly asked her if she shouldn't go for a rest. It had been a long night and she'd been busy all day. Nora had expected her to mention the 'sleepwalking' incident but she hadn't. It was typical of her aunt, not wanting to worry her. Again she noticed behind those thick glasses, the strong likeness to her mother. She felt very close to her aunt — but unfortunately it was time for another lie.

'I don't feel like lying down,' she said, 'I'd prefer to get some fresh air.'

'You're right you know,' Molly agreed. 'It'll do you all the good in the world.'

'I'll go up town for a walk,' Nora said.

'Off with you so and don't be too long. I'll be putting the tea on for your uncle soon.'

Nora made her way quickly down Church Street. Passing by Mrs Moloney's run-down house she hoped she wouldn't bump into Alec. Even if she did she wouldn't tell him where she was going. He'd done enough for Jack already and besides she was afraid he might stop her from delivering the message after what had happened to him.

Soon, she had reached the Square and at last found Foley's hardware shop. Its timber front was painted a dark, shiny blue, the surname overhead a dull yellow edged in red. Inside, the place was larger then she'd expected. There were just a handful of customers there. In fact, there were more assistants behind the various counters than customers. In one glance she noticed at least five.

She dawdled for a moment fingering a box of wax candles while trying to decide which of them seemed the most approachable. As soon as she'd ruled out a lean young man with a pockmarked face, greasy black hair and equally dark eyes, she heard a voice behind her calling.

'Vincent, I need a hand unloading these oats.'

The man she feared must be her contact stirred himself lazily and she held her breath as he opened his mean, narrow mouth.

'Vincent,' he barked, 'are you deaf or what?'

From the far end of the shop a pint-sized, jolly-looking man emerged. His red-faced smile, however, was forced and he seemed to her the type who was used to putting up with the bullying of others.

'Keep your wig on!' he chuckled but looked quickly over his shoulder like a child expecting a belt in the ear.

He came within a few feet of her.

'You'll get those candles cheaper across the road,' he whispered with an effort at cheerfulness.

'Are you Vincent Ryan?' she asked urgently.

'I am indeed and who would you be?'

She was about to tell him her name but thought better of it.

'It doesn't matter who I am,' she said. 'I have a message for you: it's important.'

'Will you stop talking,' the greasy young man shouted, 'and do what you're paid to do.'

'Why doesn't he do it?' Nora asked.

'His father owns the shop,' Vincent Ryan told her, nodding towards the door and they both went out to the street.

'I'll be with you in a minute, Jamesy,' he called to the man standing behind the ass and cart outside.

'I haven't all day now,' the man warned, lighting up his pipe.

Vincent turned to her anxiously. There were beads of sweat on his forehead. She wondered if he was bullied into this kind of thing too, taking messages from the Irregulars and passing them on. She hoped not.

'Well, what is it?'

'You're to bring the Red Setter to the Turnpike tomorrow evening.'

'Are you sure,' he said, surprise written all over his face.

'I'm sure.'

'Right,' he said. 'Away with you now and forget you ever spoke to me.'

He went about unloading the cart and laughed and joked

with the other man as she walked away. She felt strangely disappointed. Somehow, she had imagined this moment of intrigue would be much more exciting than this. Instead, it had passed off like the ordinary events in life do, without mystery.

Still there was the knowledge that she'd helped to plant the seed from which peace might grow. That knowledge helped her through the evening and the next day. Through Peter's downcast return, having failed to meet the Colonel and warned of more trouble from Captain Doyle; through the growing hints from Molly that she would have to start preparing herself to return to school; but especially through the long hours of wondering what was happening to Jack now and what he was doing. Was he, at last, doing the right things for the right reasons? Or was he powerless in the face of the angry men on both sides? Or perhaps even secretly unwilling to change the disastrous course they were all headed in? Did he still, in other words, want to die in the fight?

She struggled against her doubts until they were all too quickly confirmed in the spilled blood of another man. This time it was no stranger.

Chapter 19

The morning after the Red Setter was to be brought to the Turnpike, as Jack's message had said, Colonel O'Brien's body was found in a ditch by the roadside at that very place. A few yards away, his car stood in the middle of the road. The driver's door was still open.

An old man going to fetch water at a nearby pump stumbled upon the grim scene. He recognised the Colonel immediately. The old man had been in school with his father. He whispered a prayer in the Colonel's ear and wept bitterly all the way to the nearest farmhouse.

Within an hour of daybreak, the Colonel's remains lay in his family's house, surrounded by his grief-stricken wife and sons. The people of the town woke in confusion to hear, at such an unearthly hour, the slow insistent peal of the Dead Bell.

Peter broke the news to Molly and Nora at the breakfast table. His eyes were red from crying and his face was flushed. Molly did her best to console him as he cursed the Irregulars and, above all, Jack.

'They're animals,' he cried, 'and to think my own brother is among them.'

Nora was petrified with terror. Was it possible that the message she had delivered had sent Colonel O'Brien to his death? If it had, did this mean there was no-one left that Jack could trust? Or could it mean that Jack himself had revealed the beast that lurked behind those pale blue eyes? If this was true, the same beast was inside her too. She stared down at her hands as if she expected to see the Colonel's blood dripping from them.

'Peter,' Molly pleaded, 'you know in your heart and soul, Jack wouldn't do such a thing.'

Yes he could, Nora thought, he has killed before and a voice in her head shouted, 'Stop using that word, "killed". Murdered! Murder, is what it's called!'

Her head seemed to spin wildly, filling up with whirring, whistling noises. She clasped her hands over her ears but the screeching sounds refused to go away. She jumped up suddenly and they watched in horror as she began to scream shrilly. There were no words, only screams like the ones inside her head. She fell against the wall still screaming so as not to have to think about the awful truth or feel the beast within her.

They forgot their own misery and tried to calm her down, to no avail. Moments later, however, she did stop as the crash of shattering glass burst through the hallway from the shop. She ran to Molly and hid her face on her aunt's shoulder.

Peter went out to the shop, where the noise seemed to have come from. Soon, he returned holding a rock in his hand. Around it was tied a soiled strip of paper. He unravelled it and read the scrawled writing.

'What does it say, Peter?' Molly asked.

'One word, Molly,' he said, gravely. 'One word the De-laneys will be cursed with for all time. "Murderers!"'

Nora screamed again and fled from the kitchen to her room. She threw herself on the bed and buried her head in the pillow. Soon, the sounds and voices drifted slowly away until she was left with just her own pleading cries.

She begged her mother to forgive her, to help her. She pleaded with Jack to stop the killing. She went so far as to beg her father to come and take her from this place because nothing could be worse than this. Not his drunkenness or his threats or his open contempt of her. It filled her with anguish to feel herself driven away from the few people who really cared about her. Molly and Peter and Alec too.

She couldn't escape the feeling that she had cut herself off from her aunt and uncle by her foolish involvement with Jack. To tell them about him now would mean admitting her own guilt and this she couldn't do. That would lead to them despising her and even if, as seemed inevitable now, they must part ways, she felt she couldn't leave them on such bad terms. How could she stay with such an appalling secret on her conscience?

When Molly came to see how she was, Nora refused even to look at her.

'We mustn't think the worst,' Molly said and Nora had to bite her lip to stop from screaming again.

She couldn't understand how Molly could be so sure of Jack, especially now that he had brought the anger of some stranger crashing into their lives in the shape of a cruel word wrapped around a crude rock.

Molly stayed in the room in spite of Nora's silence. Her very presence washed away the accusing voice in Nora's mind and she slept. It was no peaceful sleep, filled as it was with guns and blood and dead men whose terrifyingly white eyes wouldn't close. Outside the wind rose and rattled the windows and banged some far-off door like an impatient caller.

Later in the evening, Nora sat on the edge of her bed. Molly had gone. On the bedside table was an untouched cup of cold tea and a slice of bread, already curling up at the corners.

At first, she was sure she merely imagined the faint swell of music. It seemed to her like the last, fading traces of a world she would never know again, of beauty and of good.

In the gathering gloom she recognised Alec's melody, sad and sweet. It was broken by the continuing bluster which carried off some notes before ever they reached her. The music stopped and started up again but always it was the same melody.

She knew Alec must be out in the hall and she had to see him. There was nothing in particular she wanted to say to him or hear him say. She simply felt that he was the last friend she had, a thought that would have been extraordinary to her not long before.

Downstairs, Molly asked if it was really such a good idea for her to go out to Alec.

'He's been hitting the bottle, Nora,' she explained. 'He's not fit company for a young girl.'

But Nora insisted. She gave no reasons, offered no excuses. She'd had enough of all that. As she walked across to the hall, the wind lashed against her and the yard seemed like some strange grey desert out of a dream. Her hair was tossed wildly and her eyes watered in the stinging breeze.

The door whipped to a close behind her but Alec remained hunched over the keys of the piano, swaying slowly from side to side as he played. On the piano-top, a faintly glowing oil lamp stood at one end. At the other, a half-empty whiskey bottle stirred, its contents lit to a yellowy gold. She was almost tempted to taste it, it looked so good, its promise of escape so reassuring.

She didn't feel she had the right any more to lecture him about the evils of drink. There were greater evils. In any case, as he'd told her once, Alec was harming no-one but himself. Perhaps that was the best you could do with your life. Go through it without harming others.

She stood at the door and tried to let the music reach inside her. Music is hope, Mrs Teehan used to tell her, it is your only true friend. But, Nora thought, you are lonely too, for all your music, Mrs Teehan.

Was loneliness to be everyone's destiny in the end? Mrs Teehan, lost in her own world, her father in his. Alec too, drunkenly lost and alone, and here, just a short walk away from him, Nora herself lost in her universe of guilt and shame.

These lost worlds seemed only to meet for an instant before drifting away from one another and circling their separate paths like planets around the sun. That warm sun which promises companionship and fellow feeling but can never be reached.

'Welcome to my wake, Nora. Only you're so young, I'd offer you a drink.'

He stopped playing and turned to face her.

'Last night,' he told her, 'I saw something that will be the end of me. I know it.'

Nora had a sudden vision of Alec watching from behind a bush as the Colonel was dragged from his car and shot.

'You saw what happened to Colonel O'Brien?' she asked fearfully.

'No, but I think I saw the men who did it.'

'Was Jack with them?'

'Of course, he wasn't,' Alec said angrily.

Her heart raced to discover hope again. Her legs felt too weak to carry her across the hall.

'But who did you see,' she cried, 'and how do you know they had anything to do with it?'

'After the pub closed last night,' he began, trying to concentrate on speaking without slurring his words, 'I went down to the river.'

'Why the river?'

'I often go there to remind myself it was there long before the town was and will be flowing long after it's gone.'

Nora was growing impatient but held back from interrupting him.

'The town, you see, and all its troubles, every town, in fact, in Ireland, in the world and every little squabble that men get themselves into, will all pass. But the rivers and mountains and the seas, will always be there. Don't you see?'

'Yes, but what about last night?'

'I was lying there on the bank of the river and I fell asleep. When I woke, the night was pitch black but I could hear two voices. Not a word of what they were saying, at first. Just the voices.'

The wind rattled the door behind Nora again and she jumped with fright. Alec's voice descended to a mutter as his chin rolled down to his chest. He straightened himself up.

'They weren't too far away,' he went on, 'maybe twenty or thirty yards. I fixed my eyes on where they seemed to be. After a few minutes one of them lit a match and held it as they both lit cigarettes.'

He shuddered and looked around the hall suspiciously as if expecting to find someone hiding in the shadows.

'One of the men was Captain Doyle and the other fellow, I didn't see his face straight off. Then just as the flame of the match went out I saw the light reflected, for an instant, on a pair of small, round spectacles. And I could see that one of the lens was broken.'

'But it was probably one of his own soldiers,' Nora said dismissively.

'I thought the same thing myself until I tried to lift myself off the ground and something snapped under my foot. They came running over and as I lay there pretending to be out for the count, it came to me.'

Suddenly Nora remembered the first time she'd seen Colonel O'Brien in the square and his conversation with Peter. The only evidence left behind by those who'd robbed the bank was a broken shard of spectacle lens!

'It was the same fellow who watched me when I was leaving Maguires. I was so bloody frightened after that day, I couldn't remember anything about him. But I realised then that I'd noticed those glasses with the broken lens.'

He shook his head in horror at his next recollection.

'They stood over me and Doyle said, "Do you think he saw us!" The other fellow told him I was probably dead drunk, to forget about it. But I could hear Doyle coming closer and anther match was struck right up by my face. He recognised me and I heard him tell the fellow with the glasses that he knew me and he'd been waiting for a chance to get me.'

As he spoke Alec was becoming more and more sober.

'I held my breath, sure it was my last one. Then the other fellow spoke up and said they'd have the whole town down on top of them if he fired a shot there and anyway there was more important work to be done that night. They went away but I was afraid to stir for hours after.'

It seemed certain now that Captain Doyle and this man with the spectacles had murdered the Colonel. Surely that was what they meant by 'more important work?' Were these two also in on the robberies together? The broken glasses and the fact that Captain Doyle's men were always conveniently out of the way during the robberies seemed to confirm this suspicion.

She herself had heard the Colonel express his doubts that the Irregulars alone were involved in the sudden spate of break-ins. What if Doyle had somehow learned of his superior's misgivings? That gave him the perfect reason to want to get rid of Colonel O'Brien.

This fellow-Irregular of Jack's must then have learned of the planned meeting with the Colonel and told Captain Doyle. The rest was easy to imagine. The only question now was whether they had shot Jack too and perhaps taken the body away from the scene.

She began to explain all of this to Alec but he didn't seem to hear. He turned to the piano again. He wasn't playing his sweet melody now. Instead, his body shook convulsively and he groaned like someone trying to ease some inner pain. She moved towards him but he stopped her with the slamming of his fists on the piano keys.

'Don't come near me,' he cried. 'I'm cursed, damned!'

She stood petrified in the centre of the hall.

'I never thought I'd have to go through such things again,' he said brokenly. 'One war is enough for any man to have to bear.'

'Please, Alec. Let me help you.'

'I'm beyond anyone's help. I'm a dead man.'

'But they don't know you saw them,' she tried to reason with him.

'Doyle is only waiting for a chance to get me,' he said, more calmly. 'Maybe I'd be better off dead anyway.'

'Everyone knows you're not an Irregular. Even Captain Doyle must know that.'

Nora inched closer as Alec began to speak in a language

she didn't understand. '... *Les morts sont tous du même camp.*'
He rocked forward and back, his arms pressed closely to his
front.

'It's French, Nora,' he said, still averting his eyes from her.
'The words of a poem written about the Great War. The Great
War! How can there be such a thing! It goes,

> *Pressing each other close, the dead*
> *Who own no hatred or flag,*
> *Their hair veneered with clotted blood,*
> *The dead are all on the same side.'*

He moved forward and pressed his forehead to the front
of the piano.

'Maybe I should have stayed over there,' he whispered. 'I
was just beginning to do what I wanted to do with my life.'

He uttered a false, empty kind of laugh.

'I was composing my own music and for a while I thought
it was bloody brilliant but it was rubbish. Nothing only
rubbish!'

'You could start again,' she encouraged him.

'With these,' he shouted, holding up his gloved hands as
he'd often done before to her.

His self-pity disgusted Nora, reminding her as it did of her
own similar feelings. It was as much herself as Alec she was
attacking as she lunged towards him and grabbed one of his
hands. He was too shocked and confused to react. She pulled
at the black glove trying to get it off. It might have been a layer
of skin, it was so tight. When it eventually slipped off she
stumbled back a step and her gaze followed Alec's, down to
what her furious action now revealed.

The hand was scarcely recognisable as that of a human
being. It was pitted and scarred. The hand of a beast. Red and

raw it was webbed with bulging purple veins. Slowly, Alec peeled off the other glove from his left hand, the hand with the stiff middle finger. Or what she thought was a stiff middle finger. The glove fell to the ground. He raised the hand. There was no middle finger. She blinked and stared again. No middle finger.

Her revulsion quickly turned to wonder that such hands could produce the most flawless music. She wanted to tell him this but at that very moment the whiskey bottle on the piano shattered and the yellow liquid sprayed out across the floor. They stared at each other dumbly and the hall echoed with another loud bang. A bullet smashed into the frame of the piano and inside the severed strings snapped with a weird, ear-splitting twang.

'Run for it!' Alec shouted and they both raced to the door.

Shots continued to fill the hall from a high window at the far end. Alec grabbed her and they set off towards the lane. As they ran he hunched over her to protect her from the shots. The heavy footsteps of their pursuer rang in Nora's ears. When they reached the yard of the house, Peter was already there. He held a gun in his hand.

'Get behind the outhouse!' he roared and began to return fire blindly into the dark lane.

The shooting soon stopped and they waited, crouched in the dark, not a word passing between them.

'They're well gone by now,' Peter said finally and guided them back to the house.

The time for secrets was over. Nora told Peter everything that had happened since she'd found Jack. As she spoke she felt the great weight of lies and deceit being lifted from her. Peter listened calmly, without a hint of annoyance and when she'd finished he sat and thought for a while in the quiet of the kitchen.

'We don't blame you, Nora,' Molly told her, 'Jack should never have involved you in the first place. He should've trusted us.'

'There's only one way to stop Doyle now,' Peter said. 'I'll have to go to Dublin and meet someone who'll take my word before his.'

'But who?' Nora said in exasperation.

'A certain Government Minister,' he explained. 'I saved his bacon back in the real fight. Now he can return the favour.'

'Doyle will be watching every move you make,' Molly objected. 'How will you get to Dublin?'

'I spent a few years on the run myself, remember. I'll leave before it gets light and pick up a car in Borris. There's a few old friends I can depend on.'

'Isn't there anything I can do?' Alec asked.

Peter handed him the gun.

'Can you use this?' he said.

Alec took his hands from his pockets and reached for it.

Molly gasped at the sight of his ravaged clumps of hands.

'I never thought they were as bad as that, Alec,' Peter said. 'How in the name of God can you play the piano at all?'

'Some would say I shouldn't bother,' Alec laughed, 'with the racket I make. Isn't that right, Nora?'

She grinned and felt strangely proud of the fact that he no longer hid his wounds. She knew it must be difficult for him.

'You're the best I ever heard,' she said and though she blushed, it was worth the small embarrassment to see him grow in confidence before her very eyes.

'By God, the compliments are flying,' Molly joked.

'I meant at the piano,' Nora added quickly. 'He has a lot to learn about good manners!'

'Enough said,' Peter smiled. 'Now, Alec, you'd better stay on guard for the night. I'll be needing a few hours' sleep.'

'I'm sorry for lying to you,' Nora said.

'Maybe it's our fault for bringing you down here in the first place,' Molly said.

Nora's desire to leave this place and return to Dublin had melted away. They had shown no anger at her deception, only concern for her.

'Don't say that,' Nora cried. 'I wouldn't want to be anywhere else.'

In that moment she felt she had found her home even if, for the present, it was in a house under siege. It was, perhaps, not a very typical family. An aunt and uncle, their niece and a stranger with war-torn hands. But all through that long, sleepless night, the bonds between them grew closer than those of any other family in the town.

Sometimes rest comes without sleep. Sometimes it comes in the growing knowledge that you have found what it is you were looking for, long after you thought it was lost forever. The certainty that you are not alone.

At five o'clock in the morning Peter left and the others sat drinking tea in the kitchen until dawn.

Chapter 20

Alec placed a finger to his lips and stole quietly along the hallway to the shop. The gun was steady in his hand. The knocking had been going on for five minutes now, growing ever more urgent. They knew it wasn't Peter. He was to come to the back door and tap twice. In any case, it was likely to be late evening or perhaps early next day before he would return. Nora and Molly waited, listening in trepidation to the insistent banging.

'It's that railwayman from Dublin,' Alec whispered from the hallway. 'The one who brings the letters from Nora's father. But there's someone with him and I can't see who it is.'

'I'll go upstairs and look down,' Molly said and went lightly up the steps.

Soon they could hear words exchanged between Molly and the pair at the door. Their voices were hushed and it was impossible to know what was being said. To Nora, however, one of the voices was unmistakable. Molly appeared at the landing, trying to force a smile.

'It's your father, Nora,' she said. 'Alec, hide the gun, will you. What'll he think if he sees it?'

'Tell him to go away,' Nora said.

'I can't do that. It wouldn't be right.'

Nora was confused. Only hours before she had convinced herself that this was her true home and these people her true family. For her that meant banishing her father from her thoughts altogether. Now, he was here disturbing her new-found peace of mind and, perhaps, threatening to destroy it altogether, as he destroyed everything else around him.

'Peter said we can't let anybody in here,' Nora cried.

'But your father came a long way,' Alec said. 'We can't leave him standing at the door.'

'It took him long enough to find me,' Nora said bitterly. 'I don't care what you do but I won't talk to him.'

The decision was left to Molly.

'We have to let him in,' she said. 'I'm sorry, Nora, but if I send him away, a time will come when you'll curse me for it.'

She nodded to Alec and he went to open the shop door. Nora felt a heave of disgust shake her as her father's rough call rang through the hallway.

'Where is my daughter? Nora! Nora!'

She moved closer to Molly. When he appeared before them Nora was shocked by what she saw. Gone was the heavy, brutish look she had grown to hate. His cheeks were hollow, his eyes too had changed. He had grown frighten-ingly thin and no longer filled out his railway clothes to bulging point as before. Only the voice remained the same and if it hadn't been for that she might actually have felt pity for him.

'Nora,' he shouted, 'I'm taking you out of this hell-hole.'

She looked at him so coldly that he turned his attention to Molly.

'I should never have let you take her from me. You and that baldy husband of yours. It's no place for a child with all this murder and mayhem around her.'

'It's not like that,' Molly said weakly.

'Isn't it all over the papers about this Colonel who was murdered,' he screamed. 'And Jimmer here told me your brother-in-law is caught up with the Irregulars. You knew when you took the child off me.'

'Now, listen here!' Alec started.

'No, you listen!' Nora's father snapped, jerking his forefinger into Alec's chest, 'I won't have it. A daughter of mine associating with a bunch of gangsters.'

'There's no Irregulars here,' Alec objected.

Nora's father tried to grab Alec but Jimmer held him back.

'I'll swing for you,' her father yelled, 'you murderers.'

'Shut up, Daddy!'

He stared at her dumbfounded. She had never challenged him like this in front of others. If she had ever protested with him it was when they were alone and his answer was always delivered in the same way — with the back of his hand. As fearful as she was now, she saw the weakness in his watery eyes.

'All you want is a maid,' she went on. 'Or maybe you want to save the few shillings you give Molly every week, so you can buy yourself more drink.'

'Shut up about the money,' he said and she was astonished at the sudden look of terror that crossed his face.

'How much did you give Molly anyway,' Nora asked harshly. 'How much was it worth to you to get rid of me?'

Nora's father turned sharply to Molly.

'If you open your mouth about this, I'll ...'

'Ah, now,' Jimmer pleaded, 'keep your head, for God's sake.'

Nora suddenly felt she had started something that might be better left alone by mentioning the money. However, she was swept along on a tide of revenge for all the hurt he'd caused her. There was no turning back from the truth, no matter how painful it might be.

'Open your mouth about what, Molly?' she demanded of her aunt. 'What does he mean?'

'I'm sure I don't know,' Molly blushed.

'Don't lie to me.' Nora cried, stepping away from her.

'You've turned her against me,' her father pleaded, 'haven't you done enough?'

Alec and Jimmer lowered their faces in embarrassment, caught up as they were in this awful family squabble. It was no place for strangers.

All at once the truth dawned on Nora. She reached out to the coat-stand for support and gripped the lacquered timber until her knuckles turned the same icy-white as her face.

'There was no money,' she said. 'It was all a big show.'

Her father's defiant glare withered away.

'With the strike and all, I ran low on funds,' he said tamely.

Jimmer looked like a man who'd just been kicked in the stomach. His mouth moved silently like that of a fish.

'I'm not worth spending a farthing on,' she accused her father. 'And now you want to rescue me from the only ones who care about me.'

He hung his head in shame. His legs sagged and Alec reached out to hold him up. Nora almost laughed at what she took to be a stupid attempt to gain their sympathy.

'Could I sit down for a minute?' he asked. 'Before I go.'

'Get out,' Nora screamed, banging her fist against the coat-stand. The pain ripped through to her elbow. 'Get out and never come back!'

'Nora,' Jimmer pleaded. 'The man's as weak as straw. He's

not been eating a blessed thing for weeks.'

'Too busy drinking, I suppose,' Nora scoffed.

'Come inside,' Molly said, 'and we'll make some tea.'

'I wouldn't give him a cup of dirty water,' Nora shouted.

'I'll make the tea,' Molly insisted, 'and we've had enough roaring and bawling for one day.'

They brought him to the kitchen but Nora stood in the doorway as they all sat down. If he'd only kept that one promise about the money she might, in time, have been able to forgive him everything else. It was the last thread between them and now it had been snapped.

Molly was cooking up some rashers and fried bread. Nora's father protested but she would have none of it. Nora couldn't understand this woman, close as she was to her. She had forgiven her father as easily as she'd kept faith with Jack.

Remembering her mother's efforts to pacify him when he flew off the handle up in Inchicore, she wanted to tell Molly that kindness was wasted on him. At the same time, she couldn't help watching his every move. She had to admit to herself that he was a mere shadow of his former, vicious self. If it was all an act it was a very convincing one.

He struggled to eat the plate of food before him. His stomach seemed to lurch with every swallow. Molly tried to keep up a hearty conversation in spite of what had just happened and her worries over Peter's safety. Jimmer too did his best to ease the tension.

'By God,' he said, 'you'd go a long way to get a rasher as tasty as that.'

Nora's father stood up suddenly from the table and lurched away through the kitchen door, brushing by Nora as if she wasn't there. In the hallway he looked around wildly, his lips tightly closed, his cheeks puffed out. He grabbed the handle of the back door and flung himself into the yard.

Without thinking, Nora rushed after him. Alec made a move to follow but Molly held his arm.

'Leave them,' she said.

When Nora found her father he was getting violently sick just outside the back door. He wavered unsteadily and she slipped her arm in around his waist.

'I'm not able to eat, Nora,' he spluttered.

Behind her, the back door slammed shut and she turned, certain it was Molly or Alec coming to help. A stranger in a long, soiled, trench coat stood there. His gun was aimed at her head. He got a grip on her free hand. From the other side, another trench-coated figure emerged and caught her father around the neck. He wore small, spectacles with one broken lens.

'Is that him?' the first stranger asked.

'No, dammit,' the bespectacled one grunted, 'he must be inside. Back away, Sean.'

They dragged Nora and her father behind an outhouse.

'What's going on?' her father cried, only slowly coming to his senses. 'Take your hands off my daughter.'

His fist, once strong, slapped weakly against the face of the one called Sean. The man's counter-punch cracked into her father's chin and he dropped slowly to his knees. Nora tried to break free but it was hopeless.

'You'll come to no harm if we get who we came for,' the man with the broken glasses said with a steely grin.

He pushed Nora roughly against the wall.

'Take it handy, Reilly,' the other man said.

Reilly stared at him as coldly as he stared at Nora. He let out a mocking laugh and turned his attention to the house. Peering around the corner of the outhouse, he called,

'Smithson! Get out here fast or we'll shoot the pair of them.'

The back door of the house opened and Molly appeared there.

'Get out of the way,' Reilly yelled.

She walked defiantly towards them.

'I'm warning you, Missus,' he said, pulling Nora out in front of him and placing the point of his gun to her temple. 'She'll get it if that drunken traitor don't come out.'

Nora was too terrified to tell him she knew it was he who was the traitor.

'I'm coming for my niece,' Molly said, 'you can threaten all you want.'

'The Free State boys picked up the Maguires this morning and that tramp in there fingered them,' he shouted.

At the back door of the house, Alec stood and held his arms aloft.

'Let the girl go,' he called.

Molly spun around and pleaded with him.

'Go back, Alec! They'll kill you.'

'Let the girl go to her aunt,' Alec repeated.

Reilly released his grip on her. She turned to help her father.

'He's all right,' Reilly said, 'we'll leave him be when Smithson gets over here.'

Nora ran to Molly's side. Alec walked by, his ungloved hands still raised.

'Did they hurt you, girl?' he asked.

Nora shook her head, unable to speak. It was unbearable to imagine she might never see him again. She wished they would take her father and leave Alec but the thought was so shameful it only made the pain worse.

'All those terrible things I said to you,' she whispered, 'I didn't mean them, Alec, I swear.'

'No apologies now, Nora,' he laughed, 'it was time someone put me in my place.'

She looked at his hands. She wanted to touch them as if her touch would somehow heal them. But it was too late for all that.

'Goodbye, Alec,' she said, sick to the pit of her stomach.

'And no goodbyes,' he added, turning with a flourish. 'I'll be back.'

As he moved closer to his captors Molly cried out,

'What right have you to do this?'

'He'll get a fair trial,' Reilly told her but his smile suggested otherwise.

'And then you'll shoot him,' Molly answered angrily.

'That's right, Missus,' Reilly laughed.

'He'll only be shot if he's proved guilty. You have my word on that, Missus,' his partner said, obviously annoyed with Reilly's attitude.

'What devil sent you to do his dirty work,' Molly asked.

'Your brother-in-law, Mrs Delaney,' Reilly announced. 'Jack!'

There was no time left to protest. Reilly had caught Alec and they were already on their way out the back lane. Nora and Molly ran to where her father lay. He groaned in pain and Nora held his bloodied head in her arms.

'Will somebody,' he asked, 'please tell me what the hell that was all about?'

They brought him inside and cleaned his wound. Jimmer had got away while the going was good. Molly explained everything to Nora's father. To Nora's surprise he didn't fly into a rage.

'I know you don't think much of me, Nora,' he said 'and I don't blame you. But the least I can do is stay here until Peter comes, in case there's any more trouble.'

She knew the Irregulars wouldn't be back now that they'd

got their man and yet she was glad he'd offered to stay.

As for Alec, she could only hope that Reilly wouldn't find a reason to kill him before they got to Jack. She couldn't understand why Jack would order his abduction but was certain he wouldn't harm Alec.

The question that bothered her most was where they had taken him. For hours she wrestled with the problem and then, later in the evening, as they waited in desperation for Peter to return, she found the answer. It was there, in the room that had once been her mother's and was now hers. There, waiting to be stumbled upon.

Chapter 21

Nora hadn't been pleased when Molly had set her to work, tidying the house from top to bottom. The ordinary chores seemed ridiculously unimportant compared to the catastrophic events going on all around her. She had made her feelings known but Molly was adamant.

'There's no point,' she insisted, 'in sitting on our tail-ends all day.'

Soon, however, it was clear to Nora that it was better to keep occupied. If you acted as if life was normal then it was easier to believe it would return to normal. To sit around in growing despair would be a kind of surrender, an admission of defeat. It helped her too to think more clearly and go beyond simply imagining the awful things that might be happening to Alec and Jack or inventing reasons why Peter might return too late or not at all.

As she swept out the spare room she remembered what Jack had said about his 'safe house'. The more extraordinary part about the secret room came to mind quickly, but was

there anything in what he'd said that might give some hint
as to where the house actually was? 'Not too far away,' he
had said.

The myriad of thoughts crowding her mind was like the
loud conversation of some seedy bar, drowning out the
words of her brief meeting with Jack. She plunged herself
even more whole-heartedly into the work and gradually the
distracting buzz filling her head died away.

'You wouldn't find better in a jungle,' she heard Jack say
and he might have been in the room with her. Then even more
clearly, something he'd told her as he'd gone on to describe
his secret place, came to her. 'The house we have in the
woods.'

By now she had reached her own room. She opened the
windows and began to fold some clothes she'd left at the end
of her bed. Putting these away, she took out some clothes that
were already folded and fixed them more neatly. She was
beginning to be afraid that soon there would be no more work
to keep her mind searching her memory for more clues. There
was nothing left to do but make the bed so she decided to
change the sheets.

She went busily down to the linen press and returned with
fresh, newly-starched sheets. Delaying this last chore for as
long as she could, she rearranged books on their shelves and
wiped the dresser she'd already cleaned, waiting for more
specks of dust to fall and sweeping them away before they
had time to settle.

At last, she turned her attention to the bed. She whipped
off the old sheets and stuffed them in a pillowcase. Setting the
fresh sheets she pulled out the bed from the wall so she could
tuck them in properly. On her hands and knees she swept
out, with a small brush and pan, the heavy layer of dust that
always seems to gather underneath beds. Reaching inside,

the brush met with something more solid than dust. She drew
the object into the light.

It was her mother's book. The one she had never quite got
round to reading. The same one, she recalled, that contained
that youthful poem of love and hope. She didn't have to read
the carefully printed words. They emerged crystal-clear from
her memory.

> *We walked along towards Templemore*
> *On a sunlit day in Spring*
> *And stopped awhile in Morley's wood*
> *To hear the young birds sing.*
>
> *And in amongst the budding trees*
> *We found a cottage bare*
> *And promised that one day we'd make*
> *Our very own home there.*

To any stranger the connection between these words and
Jack's mention of 'the house we have in the woods', would
have seemed doubtful, at the very least. Nora, however, was
convinced that her mother's cottage and his safe house were
one and the same place.

As if to confirm this, she remembered how he had told her
that her mother was the finest girl in town. She remembered
vividly the sadness in his voice on that occasion. There was,
she decided, one certain way of finding out if all this was true.

She rushed downstairs to the kitchen where her father and
Molly were sitting. They both jumped to their feet when she
burst in, certain that something was wrong. It would have
been difficult to ask her question in front of her father.

'Daddy,' Nora said, 'there's something I want to ask
Molly.'

He was taken aback and she could see he felt like an
intruder.

'Maybe I should go outside and let the two of you talk,' he said.

'It's nothing important, Daddy,' Nora told him, 'I ... I just wanted to find out which sheets to use for my bed. I'm changing them, Molly.'

'Is that all?' Molly laughed. 'Come out here to the linen press and I'll get them for you.'

'She was always a great worker,' her father told Molly, 'only I never appreciated it.'

Nora didn't have time to consider this compliment but somehow it added to the feeling inside her that everything was going to work out all right in the end.

Once outside in the hallway she brought Molly to the shop where he wouldn't hear them. She was in such a hurry that she knocked against a tin of flour. Fortunately, in spite of the loud bang when it hit the floor, it didn't spill over.

'Molly,' she asked. 'Did Mam and Jack go out together ... when they were young ... did they go for walks and ...'

It was all very embarrassing but too urgent to avoid.

'Such a question,' Molly said, covering her cheeks with her hands.

'I *have* to know!' Nora burst out, 'Alec's life may depend on it. Jack's too, maybe.'

'Are you taking leave of your senses or what?'

'Did they go out together? Tell me, please.'

'They did, Nora,' Molly sighed, 'but that was all such a long time ago.'

For a moment, the urgency of the situation gave way to curiosity. There were so many things about her mother she would never know now that she was gone. The pain of losing her was infinitely worse when she realised that in many ways her mother was a stranger to her. So much of her life was a closed book to Nora that every scrap, every small detail she could discover was of huge importance. It was a way of making her mother live again or understanding how she had lived.

'What happened that they never ... never got married,' Nora wondered aloud.

'Ah, it wasn't meant to be, Nora, that's all,' Molly said. 'When your mother ran away to Dublin she used to write to him at first and he made plans to join her. But then ... then she met your father and it was all over with Jack.'

Nora felt a twinge of the old hatred for her father but struggled against it. Would her mother, after all, have been any happier with Jack, considering the life he had chosen to live? Or perhaps he might never have joined the fight if he'd married her? The questions, she knew, were pointless, and worse they were wasting valuable time.

'Molly,' Nora whispered. 'I think I know where they're holding Alec.'

She went on to explain what Jack had told her and what lay in the lines of her mother's poem. Molly had to agree that the cottage in Morley's wood was more than likely where Alec was being held.

'But,' she said, 'Jack wouldn't harm Alec. He'll be safe there, I'm sure.'

'They're both in danger,' Nora insisted, 'that Reilly fellow is up to no good and what if he's not alone? What if some of Jack's other men are in on the robberies too?'

'We'll have to wait for Peter. He'll know what to do and this time, please God, he'll have some help with him.'

'But it might be too late then,' Nora pleaded. 'We have to do something now.'

At the doorway leading from the hallway to the shop, Nora's father stood, as yet unnoticed by the two. He cleared his throat to let them know he was there.

'Your aunt is right,' he said and it was clear he'd heard everything. 'It's best to wait for Peter.'

'You had no right to be listening,' Nora snapped.

'I'm sorry. I thought the pair of you were upstairs and I came to check the shop when I heard that noise.'

'We have to do something,' Nora shouted.

'What in the name of all that's holy can we do, only wait?'

Nora knew Molly was right but felt that common sense was a luxury she couldn't afford in this matter of life or death. She left them standing in the shop and slammed the door behind her. At the foot of the stairs she stamped loudly on the first steps so they would believe she'd gone to her room. Then she sneaked over to the back door and was away.

She ran through Church Street and over the river bridge into the Square. At Foley's shop she turned on to the Templemore road and hoped Morley's Wood wasn't too far outside town. It would only be a matter of time before they realised she'd gone. She didn't want to be caught before she found the cottage.

What she was going to do when she reached the place was something she put to the back of her mind for now. The chances of rescuing Alec on her own were too slim even to consider. Her only hope, she felt, was somehow to get Jack alone and convince him, if he needed convincing, that Alec was innocent. If Jack had some other plan up his sleeve then, at least, he could reassure her that Alec would come to no harm and that he himself would be safe too from Reilly.

None of this slowed her pace one iota. She kept herself going by imagining that she would find Jack perhaps on guard outside the cottage and would get his attention as she hid among the trees surrounding it.

A mile outside the town she met an old woman in a heavy black shawl. She felt it was safe to ask her where Morley's

Wood was but the woman raised her rough walking-stick and shouted at her.

'Get away out of that, you little scavenger and don't be bothering me!'

'But,' Nora stuttered, 'I ... I only wanted to know ...'

'I know what you're at,' the old woman squealed. 'Feckin' timber! And the likes of us out here'll be blamed for it.'

She swung her stick at Nora and it passed within an inch of her head. Nora ran on and called out over her shoulder.

'Ye oul' bag ye!'

At the turn of the road she saw, in the distance beyond the fields to her right, a tall rank of dark-green trees. She looked back along the road into town which up to this point was pencil-straight. Apart from the cantankerous old woman there was no sign of another living soul.

As she moved forward she saw that behind the column of trees there stretched, as far as the eye could see, a dense shadowy thicket of greenery interspersed with the bare limbs of other, leafless trees.

She climbed over the roadside ditch into a field. Staying close to the bushes that bordered the field she made her way quickly to the edge of the wood. There, she held her breath and listened for the smallest sound. Only the occasional singing of a far-off bird and the gentle creak of swaying trees was to be heard. She stepped into the vast shade and moved carefully into the heart of the wood. There was no going back now.

Soon, she was lost in the gloomy depths and for all she knew might simply be going round in circles. Beneath her feet, twigs snapped and each time she stood frozen to the spot for minutes on end. Finally, she decided to take her shoes off and silently enduring the sharp stabbing on the soles of her feet, she continued her search.

Another twig cracked but this time it wasn't her step which caused it. A short distance away she heard a bird screeching and rustling away up into the trees. Now the low voices of a group of men reached her ear. She took cover behind the welcome bulk of the nearest tree. Her hands were wet and clammy as she gripped the rough bark and waited for them to approach.

Though she couldn't figure out what they were saying she was sure one of the voices was Jack's. Beads of sweat glistened along the lines of her cold forehead. They were coming closer. Then she heard Jack's voice clearly. He couldn't have been more than ten yards away.

'We'll meet back at the house after dark,' he said.

Nora's eyes were closed and she expected to be discovered at any moment. Then, just as suddenly as they had come, she realised they had passed her by. She eased herself around the tree and waited until the distant hum of their conversation faded.

She went in the direction they had come from and soon came upon a well-worn path. This led, after a few short minutes, to a small clearing. There, in the one spot in this dark place where the weak, wintry sun managed to filter through, was the cottage.

Hunched down out of sight, she plucked up the courage to take a closer look. The unguarded front of the cottage, with it's half-door and a small window to each side of it, faced her. Keeping it in view she circled around to where she could see the rear of the building.

Her tread was careful but pine needles and bits of broken bark stabbed into her feet relentlessly. To her relief this side of the cottage was also unguarded. In a crouching position, like some wild, inquisitive animal, she advanced on the cottage. Her hand reached out to the roughly-plastered wall and she raised herself from the undergrowth.

Standing quite still with her back firmly against the wall, she listened. There was no sound. Within arm's reach on both sides of her were the back windows. Her heart raced as she turned her head slowly around the edge of one and then the other. Both were empty. She couldn't see through the front windows which meant there were at least two further rooms in the front part of the cottage.

She crawled stealthily around the windowless side of the cottage. From below the sill of one of the front windows she raised her head and immediately skulked down again. The Irregular called Sean was sitting opposite Alec in there. He had a gun in his hand. She was certain neither of them had seen her.

In that quick, fearful glance she had noticed no big fire-place like the one Jack had described. The other window had to be the kitchen window.

From afar came the heavy trudge of footsteps along the path towards the cottage. She tried desperately to open the window but it wouldn't budge. The sounds came nearer and nearer. She picked up a stone and pitched it high over the roof so it would land in the trees behind the cottage. However, it didn't quite reach that far. Instead, it thundered off the roof at the rear of the cottage, rolled down noisily along its steep pitch until it fell with a bang on the window sill of one of the back rooms and skittered away into the undergrowth.

Alec's captor rushed in to the back room to see what was happening and Nora slipped open the half-door and made it into the kitchen without being seen. She dashed to the open fireplace as the Irregular raced to the front door and ran out, cocking his gun, into the clearing.

Her fingers trembled violently as she searched for the catch of the secret door, wondering if she was mad to have believed Jack's story. She lurched back into the shadows of the fireplace as the man's shadow passed by the kitchen window. Her hands raced desperately up and down the left side of the wide fireplace. A sooty dust rose to her nostrils and she held her breath trying not to sneeze. Her search becoming more frantic she felt along the length of the other side. A few inches from the floor a jagged piece of metal scratched into her palm. She twisted and turned her blackened fingers to get a grip on it. Little more than a foot above the ground she found the smallest of handles and turned it. The secret door slid open and she slipped inside, closing it softly behind her.

There were loud murmurings for a long while from the next room but soon the cottage fell silent. In the dark, cramped space, Nora barely had room to sit. Her knees pressed against her shivering body, she inhaled the stifling odour of black fear in the coal dust. She was seized by a terrible dread that this narrow dark chamber could be home to all manner of insects or four-legged creatures. But there was a greater fear. If it had been difficult to get into this place, surely getting out would be next to impossible? In the pitch-dark she tried to find the handle on the inside of the secret door. She had to straighten up a little so that her hand could reach down below. As she did so she saw that there was a tiny peep-hole which she could reach at an uncomfortable stretch. Through it barely a ray of light entered. However, when she looked out she realised that she could see into the kitchen.

What she couldn't see was that on the other side of the secret door an inch of her dress, caught in her frenzied hurry, was clearly visible to anyone who thought to look.

Chapter 22

The light in the kitchen soon waned and Nora, in her hiding-place, stared at a point far above her where an opening, no larger than a chimney pipe, revealed a single star from the night sky. Surely, she thought, Peter was back from Dublin by now and was, perhaps even now, making his way here. She had been foolish to rush into the woods but there was no point in dwelling on that now. At least here, there was the faint hope that she might yet be able to do something for Alec and Jack too.

In the next room there was another flurry of activity. Muffled voices, sounds like chairs scraping across floors and other dull thuds whose causes she tried to keep herself from imagining. A door squeaked open close by and at once the kitchen was filled with a wavering light casting long shadows across the floor.

'Bring him in here,' Jack's unmistakable voice ordered.

He sat down at a table by the window and set the oil lamp there. The lines of worry on his face were exaggerated by the light shining from below him. His paleness seemed almost devilish, it glowed so brightly out of the sinister gloom. 'He's a good man,' Nora told herself repeating Molly's words like they were a prayer.

A chair was brought to the other side of the table. Alec, with his hands tied behind his back was dragged over and shoved on to it by Reilly.

'Take it handy,' Jack said sharply, 'There's no need for that.'

'After all the lies he's been telling about me,' Reilly said, 'he's lucky I don't plug him right here.'

'You know it's the truth,' Alec shouted and then bowing his head, pleaded with Jack. 'For God's sake, Jack, will you not believe me?'

Reilly planted a fist into Alec's face. Alec fell heavily to the ground. Jack moved his right hand inside his jacket and brought out a gun. He rested his elbow on the table and pointed the gun at Reilly.

'Pick him up,' he ordered.

'Let him crawl on the floor like the worm he is,' Reilly answered. Jack straightened himself up and raised his gun.

'I won't tell you a second time!' he said.

Reilly hesitated and then grabbed Alec's shoulder. He placed him back in his chair, a little more carefully this time. He glared maliciously at Jack.

'When are you going to make up your mind what you're going to do with him?' Reilly shouted angrily.

'I already have,' Jack told him and braced himself for what was to follow.

'Alec Smithson,' Jack went on. 'You know the charges against you. You're accused of being an informer. How do you plead?'

Alec lifted his bruised face and looked defiantly around

him until eventually fixing his gaze on Jack.

'You know as well as I do,' he said quietly, 'I told no-one about the Maguires or about the Parnell Hall. Why would I do that and then take your place? Doyle might have shot me.'

He turned to Reilly.

'Isn't that right?' he asked him sarcastically. 'You know him better than anyone else here.'

'Don't touch him, Reilly!' Jack warned and continued. 'I don't know why or how you did it but you betrayed us, Alec.'

'Jack!' Alec pleaded.

'You betrayed us and I have no alternative but to ...'

Nora gasped in horror in her hiding-place.

'But to order your execution.'

At that moment he looked towards the fireplace and Nora felt he was staring into her very eyes. He stood up suddenly and headed towards her. Nora drew her face back from the peep-hole. Very close by, she could hear him call.

'I heard a noise out there! Sean, take him into the other room. Reilly, Seamus, get out and see what's going on.'

A door slammed shut and within seconds she was face to face with Jack. He had seen the tell-tale inch of cloth.

'Nora!' he whispered. 'What the hell are you doing in here?'

'You can't do this to Alec,' she cried. 'You can't.'

'Keep your voice down,' he told her. 'Of course, I won't kill him. I'm going to take him into the woods and let him go.'

'But what about you?'

'I have to stay here and convince the others that Reilly is our real enemy,' he said. 'If only I could find out where he's hiding the money. That would be proof enough.'

They heard the others coming back and Jack closed the secret door carefully.

'Don't worry,' he said quietly through the peep-hole, 'I'll

get you out of there.'

Reilly burst into the kitchen.

'I thought I heard voices in here,' he said suspiciously.

Jack was still on his knees at the fireplace. Nora could see his face and though his answer was, she supposed, a lie she was convinced there was some truth in it.

'I was saying a prayer, Reilly,' he said. 'May God forgive me for what I have to do.'

'You're going to do it yourself then?' Reilly answered. 'You know I'd be only too glad to.'

'I don't expect anyone to do what I wouldn't do myself.'

'So when are you going to plug him?'

'This very minute,' answered Jack. 'Sean will come with me. You two can stay and keep an eye on the place.'

'But, Jack ...'

'That's an order,' Jack interrupted. 'And as long as I'm in command you do what I say!'

Jack left the kitchen and from the next room could be heard the sound of a scuffle as they dragged Alec out into the night. Nora looked upward to that one shining star but it had disappeared behind a cloud.

As she waited for it to return she imagined herself to be in a vast meadow where she could stretch out her arms and legs and walk, run, do anything she wanted to do. In the meadow she saw Alec and Jack, Peter and Molly, her father and brothers. Best of all, she saw her mother, smiling and young, sitting in a far-off corner writing her poems under the wide shade of an oak tree. Soon, however, the darkness consumed her again.

Reilly was talking in sinister tones.

'I don't trust him, Seamus,' he said. 'He's too pally with that Smithson fellow. I don't believe he'll plug him.'

'He's a hard man when he wants to be,' Seamus replied.

'Hard, my back!' Reilly went on. 'He's on to us, I'm sure of it. I met Doyle last night and he says we have to get rid of him quick before he lands the three of us in trouble.'

'Can't we just take the money and disappear?' Seamus said in desperation. 'I didn't join up for this thieving or for sending the likes of the Maguires to jail.'

'It had to be done,' Reilly told him. 'We had to stick something on Smithson.'

'It's not right, Reilly.'

'Look, you're up to your neck in this, Seamus. There's no way out of it only to get rid of Jack. We'll be meeting Doyle at the Turnpike as soon as we finish him off. We're to split the money tonight.'

'He's the one I don't trust, Reilly,' Seamus said.

'Don't worry, we'll be plugging him too. Then the cash will be ours.'

A single shot rang out in the distance and Nora put her hands to her ears. Jack and Sean would be back at any minute and she couldn't think what to do next. If she showed herself now, she would surely be shot like the others. If she did nothing, they would walk straight into Reilly's trap.

Before she had time to decide, the kitchen door squeaked open again. Reilly and Seamus readied themselves. They waited for Sean to move in from the door. Reilly stepped around behind him, closed the door and crashed his pistol against Sean's head. Seamus caught him before he hit the floor. Reilly peered out by the window.

'No sign of him yet,' he whispered, his lips slavering with the taste of revenge to come. 'I'll be taking no more orders from him!'

Seamus took out a length of rope from a trunk and began to tie up Sean. Reilly was still at the window with his back to Nora's hiding place.

'Soon as I catch sight of him, he's a dead man,' he snarled. 'Then you can plug Sean.'

'Can't we just leave him, Reilly,' Seamus said weakly, still busy with his rope.

'And hang ourselves? I'll do it myself if I have to,' Reilly warned him.

Nora knew this was her last chance to act. Whatever the danger, it was better than sitting there waiting for another, more fatal shot to be fired.

Turning the handle of the secret door she counted to three and suddenly burst out in to the room. Heading straight for Reilly she gathered all her strength and as he was about to turn around she smashed his face into the glass of the window.

Seamus leaped towards her but bumped heavily into Reilly who was reeling away from the window with blood seeping between the fingers gripping his face. Nora threw open the door and raced outside. She heard the crunching sound of boots in the undergrowth and headed towards it. She looked back as she ran to see if either of them was yet following and tumbled over a broken branch. A sharp pain shot through her weak ankle. She got to her feet and struggled on.

'Nora!' Jack called from the shadows before her.

'They're going to kill you Jack,' she cried out as he came alongside her. 'You and Sean! He's tied up inside. We have to run!'

A bullet stabbed into the bark of a tree not more than four feet away.

'Come on, girl!' Jack shouted and grabbing her arm, pushed her away into the thicket behind him. 'Get out of here!'

'But what about you?'

Her eyes stung with tears of pain as she pleaded with him.

'I'm not leaving Sean in there,' he said. 'The game is up for Reilly now, for all of us. I have to see it through. Now go or they'll ...'

A sickening crack like that of some ancient tree splitting before its fall, tore through the wood. Jack gasped in mid-sentence and dropped to his knees. He fell into Nora's arms.

'Jack!' she screamed, 'Jack!'

'Nora,' he whispered. 'I only did what I thought was right.'

His head rolled back and she shook him violently, screaming at him not to die but was already too late. Two more shots shattered the momentary silence that fell on her when she realised he was gone. She lay his head to rest and limped away desperately trying to hurry but weakening with every step. She heard Reilly's voice nearby.

'There he is!' he shouted. 'We got him!'

'What about the young one?' Seamus called.

'We'll find her,' Reilly roared menacingly, making sure she could hear him.

'Let her go, can't you?'

'Go back to the cottage and watch Sean, you useless coward.'

Nora plunged on into the tree-filled depths. Once again she tripped over some unseen debris. Every part of her ached — her body with the agony of her twisted ankle, her mind with the horror of Jack's death. She couldn't find the strength to lift herself. All she could think of in her worn-out state was how little time there had been from the moment he was hit to the moment he passed away. There was no time to say she believed he wasn't an evil man or to say that she loved him better than her own father and how she wished he and her mother had stayed together.

She felt herself drifting away and for a strange instant she seemed to be looking down on herself from somewhere above in the trees. Up there watching, in a calm detached way, her own crumpled body and the fast-approaching Reilly skulking through the maze of trees.

Without warning a hand pressed itself around her mouth and another eased forward into view, its fingers gripping the handle of the pistol. The shot exploded in Nora's ears and she heard Reilly hit the ground.

'Seamus!' he yelled fearfully, 'I'm hit.'

Nora looked into the face of her rescuer.

'I never fired one of these yokes in my life,' her father said.

'Daddy!' Nora cried, the thoughts of the previous moments flooding back to her, 'I'm sorry.'

'Quiet, Nora,' he whispered. 'We're not out of this yet.'

They listened to the rustling noise of Reilly crawling back towards the house. From behind came more crackling footsteps and Nora's father spun around.

'Don't come a step closer,' he warned but all around the woods were filled with the unmistakable sounds of a large group advancing on them.

'Jim,' came the answer. 'It's Peter.'

They both breathed a sigh of relief as Peter stalked to their side. He was followed by at least ten soldiers in Free State uniforms.

'But they're Doyle's men, Uncle Peter,' Nora gasped.

'They're taking orders from me now,' Peter said firmly. 'Is Jack in there?'

'He's dead!' Nora burst out. 'Reilly shot him. He's over there.'

Peter's lower lip quivered in rage.

'I'll kill him!' he roared and struggling away from the grip of one of the soldiers, he made for Reilly who was still scuttling away like a wounded animal. Within seconds, Peter was upon him.

'You can't shoot me,' Reilly whimpered. 'I ... I lost my gun back there. You can't shoot me.'

Peter lowered his pistol to the man's head.

'You murdered my brother.'

The soldiers and Nora's father now stood around the pair. In spite of her pain, Nora reached them and broke through the circle. They were pleading with him not to pull the trigger.

'There's enough rough justice in the country as it is, for Heaven's sake! You don't want his blood on your hands for the rest of your life,' Nora's father told him.

'Shut up, the lot of you!' Peter shouted. 'I've stayed quiet long enough and look where it's got me. My brother's dead and someone has to pay for it.'

His finger tightened on the trigger. Reilly closed his eyes. Nora limped forward and touched the trembling hand holding the gun. She eased it away from Reilly's head. Tears rolled down Peter's face and she held him as he sobbed quietly to himself.

She told the soldiers about the two Irregulars who were still in the cottage and asked if they'd found Alec but no-one had seen him. They moved forward and surrounded the cottage. It wasn't long before Seamus threw his gun out into the clearing and emerged with his hands above his head. Inside, Sean still lay bound and unconscious on the kitchen floor.

Peter had recovered by now and along with Nora's father went in search of Alec. They called his name continuously but there was no answer. It was Nora who stumbled over his body and fell right alongside his bloodied head. She screamed and scrambled away from him on her hands and knees.

'He's breathing,' Nora's father said.

'Alec,' Peter said. 'You're all right, we'll get you back to town.'

Nora heard Alec moan and forced herself to turn and look. His eyes were opening.

'I ...' he tried to speak. 'I ...'

Peter threw off his jacket and ripped away the sleeve of his shirt to clean the wound on Alec's forehead.

'I ...' Alec muttered. 'I couldn't see where I was going and I ... I ran into a tree.'

If the circumstances had been different they might all have laughed but Nora was beside herself with anger.

'You fool,' she shouted. 'You stupid, stupid man! You frightened the life out of me.'

'Nora,' her father objected. 'Can't you see he's in a bad way?'

'I thought he was ...' Nora murmured. 'You fool, Alec. Thank God, you're alive.'

'I feel better already,' Alec groaned and twisted his face into a smile.

They brought him to the road where an army lorry was waiting. On the way she told Peter what she'd heard Reilly say about meeting Captain Doyle at the Turnpike.

Back in town, Nora was disappointed when Peter absolutely insisted that she wouldn't be going out there for the last act of that long, terrible day. She felt it was unfair and said so but Peter was not to be moved. As far as he was concerned she had seen enough danger and there was no knowing how Doyle would react when he found himself trapped like the rat he was. When Peter had left Molly finally persuaded Nora to go to bed.

'As soon as we get word from the Turnpike,' she assured her, 'we'll be up straight away to tell you.'

Nora no longer had the energy to protest. Alec had

checked out her ankle in spite of his own injuries and told her there was nothing to worry about. It hadn't been broken again but it hurt so badly she was glad to give in to his pleas and lie on her bed.

'I keep thinking I could have done more,' she told him, 'or maybe I tried to do too much.'

'You did more than anyone had a right to expect,' he said.

As she lay there she wondered if returning to Dublin was the only way she could forget the events of these past weeks. She wished, above all else that her mother would give her some sign, some hint of what she should do next.

The gentlest of knocks sounded on her bedroom door. Her father entered quietly and came to the bedside. At first she kept her eyes closed as their breaths came and went, swapping places in the still heart of the night. The sounds fitted together perfectly like the left and right hands in a rolling waltz. She never felt so close to him. She opened her eyes. He was crying.

'You look so like your mother,' he said.

'I could come back home with you, Daddy,' she told him. 'I don't really belong here.'

'And I'd have you back in the morning if I thought it was the right thing to do.'

'I want to come back.'

'Maybe you do now, Nora,' he said. 'But what's up there for you? Nothing. No more than there was for your mother. You'd have to go out working or spend the time slaving away in that little house with no chance of ever using your talent or ...'

'I don't care about music,' she objected weakly.

'Of course you do. And what's more your mother's heart was set on it for you. I did my best to stop you back then but I won't let you give it up now.'

'This isn't my home,' she said, only half-believing her own words. 'I could never be happy here.'

'You were never happy in Inchicore and that was all my doing,' he admitted. 'Look, Nora, these are good, decent people and things will be settling down here now. They'll give you the chance you deserve to make a go of the music. That's something I can't do for you.'

It was clear that he'd made up his mind before he'd even reached her room. This time, however, he had made his decision only with her in mind.

'What will you do up there on your own?' she asked.

'I was never a loner, Nora,' he smiled. 'Maybe I'd have been better off if I had been. Besides, it's only a few hours on the train and I'm not making any idle promises now, I'm just telling you, I'll be down here every chance I get to see you.'

'I know you will,' she said, glad to have a father she could believe in and who had been there when she needed him, alone in the wood.

Soon, Peter arrived back from the Turnpike with the news that Doyle had surrendered without a shot being fired. Now Reilly and Doyle were busily blaming each other for all the robberies. It transpired that they had been friends in Mullingar and that a number of robberies in that area before the troubles began had never been solved. When Doyle had been transferred to Colonel O'Brien's command, Reilly had contacted him and they'd taken up their old ways. Neither of them would admit to firing the fatal shot on the Colonel but it was clear they were equally responsible no matter which of them pulled the trigger.

It was all over and Nora could begin to settle in to that new life that had seemed for so long to be just around the corner. But nothing is quite that simple. Happy endings are a long time coming — if they come at all.

Chapter 23

Although peace returned to the town and surrounding villages very quickly, another three long months passed before the Irregulars laid down their arms countrywide. Day by day, week by week, the newspapers in their shop reported fewer incidents, each one further away. Jack's squad of men wasn't replaced and so the bridges and roads were soon clear of all damage.

For the townspeople it was a strange time. There was no sign of trouble and yet the large military force remained as a painful reminder of what had happened. People were troubled now only by a sense of guilt that others, admittedly fewer by the day, didn't have it so easy. For many there were the memories of loved ones lost and the scars in body and soul that had to be lived with for long years to come.

It was an uneasy time too for Nora. Her father was to be seen striding up Church Street to Stannix Lane more and more often now, looking healthier than he'd ever done. Nora, however, hadn't quite convinced herself that it was right for her to have so easily accepted his insistence on her remaining in town.

It didn't seem right either that she should allow herself to feel even remotely happy while Jack lay in the cold earth up at St Patrick's Cemetery. When she saw the sun or the first buds of spring or a perfect, cloudless sky, she couldn't help thinking he would never see these things again.

She worried too about her brothers in America. Her father told her that Uncle Phil had written and that they were settling down well. She felt a little hurt at first when she'd heard this but she soon realised that, like her, they too must have their moments of regret. What could they do but make the best of things as she herself was trying to do? She could only hope that one day they would all meet again.

In Peter and Alec also she sensed this terrible unease. They were both very quiet in themselves. If it hadn't been for Molly they might all have lingered forever in the hell of despair.

She dragged a reluctant Nora down to school for her first day and insisted, in spite of her protests, that she start immediately with a new music teacher there. The piano in the Parnell Hall was still in a mess after the bullets which had splintered its timbers and shorn off half its strings. Nora promised to work on the school piano. She couldn't face going back into the hall.

Molly introduced her to two girls who lived nearby and encouraged them to call to the house. In time, Aine and Siobhan, became her closest friends. At first, however, she let them know in no uncertain terms that she could do without friends. It was too difficult for Nora to forget how easily you can be cut off from those close to you.

Alec and Peter were spurred into action by Molly. First, she set them to repair the hall's broken windows and timbers and bullet-riddled plaster. She found work in the house for them and in the shop. If they objected she scolded them like children and told them she was damned if she was going to work herself into the ground while they moped around the place.

When she had busied all of them with these everyday things that keep people going in life, she announced her grand plan. A plan that she hoped would raise all their lives above the ordinary again.

At the kitchen table she looked around at the three glum faces surrounding her. Nora was back from school where she'd had a row with a girl who'd made fun of her Dublin accent. It wasn't so much her anger with the girl that upset her but the memory it brought of Jack who'd remarked on her accent when she was nursing him in the hall. It seemed the past would never be allowed to fade from her memory.

Though her new friends had defended her she'd argued with them too. She had stormed away home alone, refusing to walk with them. Alec and Peter had been on the roof, repairing some broken tiles. Alec had belted himself on the thumb with his hammer. Peter's hat had fallen down into the street and when he went to search for it, the thing was nowhere to be found. It was no place for cheerfulness but Molly wasn't put off by such minor mishaps.

'The only true happiness is in making other people happy!' she said grandly.

They looked at her as if she had broken into some strange, incomprehensible language.

'You've been drinking again,' Alec said sarcastically.

Peter and Nora sniggered. This was the nearest thing to a laugh they had managed for quite a while.

'Isn't it grand to see you all laughing?' Molly went on. 'But am I right or what?'

'I suppose,' Nora said and turned to Peter.

He seemed already to have understood what was on Molly's mind.

'Molly, I told you already,' he said firmly, 'I'm finished with all that business.'

'People need a bit of joy in their lives,' Molly insisted. 'Something to look forward to.'

'Huh!' Peter grunted. 'The same people who threw a rock in our shop window and called us murderers?'

'That was one bad apple, Peter. You know what they say about that.'

'To hell with the lot of them.' Peter said.

'Can't you see,' Molly pleaded, 'that painting them all with the one brush is doing the same thing as that person who threw the rock? Making wild judgements about others.'

'How could you even think about it after all we've been through?' Peter said in exasperation.

'If ever there was a time to open the cinema,' she said finally, 'surely to God, this is it, when we all need a bit of a lift.' They hummed and hawed and no decision was reached that evening. Molly, however, wasn't about to let them off the hook. Every chance she got she dropped hints until it became like torture for them. They soon realised that there wouldn't be a minute's peace for any of them if they didn't give in. She even enlisted Nora's father to support her plan. Now, each time he visited he would go on about what a great idea it was.

In the end Peter relented and Nora agreed reluctantly to take her part, as did Alec. Molly thought they should go ahead straight away. At a push, she said, they could be ready in a week. Peter was adamant that if they were going to do it they'd do it right. That would mean, he reckoned, at least three weeks.

'If we went ahead in a week,' he explained, 'we'd have to make do with some old picture we've had already. I want to

book something new and that'll take a bit of time. We'd have
to bring it down from Dublin ourselves.'

Molly didn't argue. She had sown the seed and was now
prepared to wait patiently for it to grow.

The first thing Peter did was to repaint the sign for the
Stella Cinema. His spirits lifted even as he worked on it. When
he'd finished it was brighter than ever before. Soon, he had
Mick from the garage working on the generator and after a
few frustrating nights of filling the yard with their curses,
they got it running smoothly.

On his next visit, Nora's father agreed to call to the agent
in Phibsboro about the films. He would bring them down on
the big night and take them back the following day. Peter
hired a car from Mick and he and Alec went to Limerick to
get strings for the piano.

The curses raining down on the generator the previous
week were nothing to those pouring from Alec as he went
about fixing the piano. The air was blue with his oaths and
he added some in French for good measure. It was the first
time in months that Nora gave in to the humour of the
moment.

For the best part of a week, Alec struggled with replacing
the old strings and tuning the new ones.

'If only I had my gloves,' he complained every five minutes. 'I'm sure I could work better with those blasted things
on me.'

There was little he or Peter could do with the body of the
piano. The truth was, the thing looked as if it might fall apart
at the slightest touch. But it was made of sturdy stuff, with a
cast-iron frame beneath the heavy timber. It would have
taken more than mere bullets to silence it forever.

Peter, Molly and Nora stood around Alec as he sat down,
at last, to coax some music from the restored instrument. It

seemed to lift the curse that had been hanging cloud-like over the hall. Their wonder increased beyond all imagining at the sight of the nine fingers of Alec's two scarred hands playing impossibly before their very eyes.

The melody which Nora regarded as somehow her own, though she'd never played it, sang with perfect clarity through the bright hall. The gentle, heart-rending opening seemed to say, 'yes, we have known sadness,' and 'yes, we may know sadness again' but slowly the chords began to brighten like the promise of better things to come.

'Molly,' Peter called above the swelling music. 'Will you dance?'

'I will, sir,' she laughed.

She raised her hand and he held it and bowed. They walked away and Alec raised the volume as they were tossed on the rolling waves of the melody. Nora clapped them aloud and laughed as Peter stumbled into the chairs behind them.

'Mind my toes,' Molly grinned.

They weren't the world's best dancers but at that moment it only mattered that they danced. Soon they were all lost in a world where there was no anger or violence, no right causes, no wrong actions, no sorrow and no death. In a flood of quickly-forgotten embarrassment, Nora was called in to dance with Peter until finally he gave up the ghost and Molly and Nora finished out the waltz together.

Alec stood up and took their applause. As they clapped Nora thought the two weeks would never pass before the Stella Cinema would open its doors again. It felt good to be looking forward to the future.

Peter and Molly having got their breath back left the hall humming the melody between them as they went.

'You'd think they'd just met,' Alec smiled when they were gone. 'A right pair of lovebirds they are.'

Nora hardly noticed what he was saying. She wanted to
know more about the melody. Before now, there was always
something in the way of her asking him.

'Alec, who wrote that piece?'

'Ah, some French fellow,' he said. 'I don't even know what
it's called. I was probably drunk when I learned it.'

'Could you teach it to me?'

'I'll see if I can find the sheet music for you. It's not very
good anyway.'

As he spoke his mind seemed to be elsewhere. She noticed
a brightness in his eyes she had never seen before. He looked
young again. Almost boyish.

'Nora,' he continued after a while. 'Just now when I was
playing and you were all dancing, I felt like I did years ago.
I felt I could do what ever I wanted and there were no
obstacles in the way. Nothing at all to stop me only fear. But,
Nora ...'

He opened out his hands and stared at them.

'I'm not afraid any more!'

She was glad to hear him talking like this but if he truly
meant what he'd said then his next course of action was clear.

'Are you going back to France then?' she asked.

He began to pace around the hall, rubbing his hands
together, stopping abruptly and moving on again.

'I don't know, but whatever happens I don't want to lose
this feeling.' It seemed better not to ask any more questions.
She left him in the hall and went outside. She didn't want to
think about the possibility of Alec leaving or even admit to
herself that it mattered in the least to her.

Instead, she recalled every moment of the dance and ran
back to the house, to Peter and Molly. She would let nothing
disturb her new sense of contentment. But, in the back of her
mind she was prepared for the worst. It was a hard habit to

break.

The next afternoon she returned to an unusually quiet house. Her doubts had been confirmed. Not only had Alec decided to go but he had already gone. Molly told her she'd found two envelopes slipped under the shop door when she'd opened up earlier in the morning. One was addressed to Peter, the other to Nora.

In the letter to Peter, Alec apologised for letting them down. He had added that he had no choice but to leave straight away.

'While the feeling was on him,' he wrote. Molly told Nora. 'I don't understand what he meant by that!'

Nora knew quite well but it didn't make it any easier for her. She went to her room holding her own envelope. She stared at it a long while before she found the strength, at last, to open it.

Dear Nora,

I know that as you're reading this letter you'll be thinking how I've let you all down and not for the first time. I'm sorry to have to leave at all and especially with the great plans Molly and Peter had for the cinema. If I was any other man I'd have stuck it out for the two weeks but I know myself too well to delay any longer. I'm certain I would have ended up in Donnelly's pub, dreaming about what I might have done.

I'm not running from anything — rather I'm going towards my true destiny. I mean to compose again and for me, Paris is the place to do that.

Now, I'm asking a last favour of you. Perhaps you've already done enough for me, starting with that smack in the gob down in Donnelly's! I think that made me slowly begin to come to my senses.

This is the favour. Will you take my place at the cinema in two weeks? I wouldn't ask if I thought it was beyond you. If you can't do it for me, then do it for Molly and Peter.

I seem to remember that you learned five or six pieces from my collection in the piano-stool. You'll find they'll get you through. There's another piece you'll find there that will cover you for the quicker action. It's more difficult but you'll find it worthwhile. I always felt you didn't regard the other pieces as 'real music'. Am I right? In any cases try to learn pages three to six of Beethoven's *Appassionata* which I've left on top of the piano for you.

I've also written out that melody for you, the one you asked about. You might find some use for it. I'll enclose it with this letter.

One day I'll be back with music worthy of your talent. In the meantime, do forgive me, but I'm still too much of a coward for goodbyes.

Your friend, Alec.

Nora was still overcome by his words an hour after reading them. It seemed to her that he over-estimated her ability by a long shot. She unfolded the second sheet of paper and saw printed out carefully the quavers, minims and crochets of its familiar strains. Emblazoned across the top, in large letters were the title and the name of the composer:

   Melody for Nora by Alec Smithson.

This was a greater surprise than anything the letter had contained. She felt the stirring of a huge emotion and decided there and then to go to the hall and play the piece. Somehow, she knew that if she didn't go right away she might never be able to bring herself to play it or anything else on the piano, ever again.

In the hallway below she ran past Molly, unable to speak. For three hours she worked at the piece ignoring Molly's call to tea. Ignoring too the voice in the back of her head that told her never to make a friend, that friends always leave you or you will have to leave them, that happiness is always taken away, that music is only a lie, a pretence that joy is possible.

By the time she'd mastered the last line of Alec's melody, her melody, she had made her decision. Molly and Peter were speechless with gratitude and not a little concerned for the task she had set herself. Deep down, they doubted that she could play for the pictures with so little time to prepare. However, they didn't dare say so.

'It's something I have to do,' she said.

What she didn't say was that she was going ahead with this only partly for them. Her real reasons had more to do with herself. It was a kind of selfishness, she supposed, but as Rosie Tobin had once said, sometimes you have to be selfish.

She wanted to prove that she wasn't powerless in the face of the huge forces that seemed to drag so many people down and make their lives miserable. Forces like those which had robbed her mother of all her dreams. Forces that had, in the end, beaten Jack in spite of his courage and his high ideals.

Alec and, in his own small way, her father had shown her how these forces which threatened to engulf you could be overcome. It wasn't a question of changing the world as Jack and, perhaps, her mother had once believed. Rather, it was a

matter of changing yourself, of turning away from the past
and self-pity, from all those things that blinded you to your
own uniqueness, your own talents and strengths. She would
test the limits of her own ability.

On that opening night, two weeks later, it was as if time
had for a few blissful hours paused for breath. From the
moment Peter introduced his new 'musical accompanist', as
he called her, to the crescendo of applause at the end of the
'big picture', she was transported to a state of hypnotic rap-
ture.

The intense concentration and discipline of her preparation had, as soon as she touched the keys, thrown open the
door to a new freedom. She felt that she had taken command
of her own life and would never again be a slave to the tyrant
of misfortune.

Her father was there, cheering at the back of the hall and
Mrs Teehan too, whom he'd brought along to surprise Nora.
He wasn't the heartless father of old and even Mrs Teehan
wasn't pining in her loneliness. Her red cheeks glowed with
satisfaction and pride as she spoke.

'I knew you could play better than any pupil I've ever
come across but tonight I saw that you can *perform*,' she said.
'Tomorrow, I'll be meeting your new music teacher: there are
plans to be made.'

'But I made mistakes,' Nora said modestly.

'Even your mistakes were brilliant!' Mrs Teehan enthused.

~

In the months and years that followed Nora came to discover
increasingly how these words held the key to a way of life.
You don't stop dead in the middle of a piece of music just
because you've made a mistake. In the same way you don't

stop living because things are not working out as you'd hoped. If you don't make mistakes you never learn anything. Imperfection is not a barrier to fall before but an opportunity to use strength and courage in sweeping it away.

She reminded herself frequently that all imperfections are not as glaring as Alec's ravaged hands. But we have them nonetheless. The thing to remember, Nora knew, was that everyone had their own Paris or their Tipperary town where they could begin their life-long task of overcoming these imperfections.

For now, Nora had found hers.

NEW FROM MARK O'SULLIVAN

WASH-BASIN STREET BLUES
Nora in New York

The omens are foreboding, even crossing the Atlantic. Whose is the frightening face pressed against the window as Nora plays the grand piano aboard ship? Why does she distrust her new aunt Fay? Just who is betraying who?

Here is the mystery she must solve. A metallic clanging sound disturbs Nora's dreams, turning them into nightmares. A net of fear and violence is closing in.

On its own or as a sequel to the highly acclaimed *Melody for Nora*, *Wash-Basin Street Blues* is a chilling action-packed novel.

'An unusual and imaginative read' Books Ireland on *Melody for Nora*.

Melody for Nora was shortlisted for the 1995 Bisto Book of the Year Award.

LAND OF DEEP SHADOW
Pat Hynes
This is the story of Packo, a hare who takes up the challenge of the Prophecy — an ancient epic tale sending him on a journey fraught with danger: preying owls, packs of squirrels and the need for wily cunning and breakneck speed to outwit and outrun the hunting hounds. But in his gruelling trek to the *Land of Deep Shadow*, Packo learns why he is not like other hares — why he alone must stand apart. £3.99

AN ECHO OF SEALS
Romie Lambkin
The summer world changes unexpectedly for Aideen and Ben. A wounded seal is rescued by the mysterious Mr Carrigan who invites the cousins to watch the night sky through his telescope. But what does he really want them to see? What is the secret of the seals? £3.99

IT'S PIN BIN DIM DOMINILLI!
Cormac MacRaois
Jim and Caitríona Doran have never seen a Dominillo until Pin appears the day before their birthday. 13 centimetres of mischief, he steals biscuits, bewilders the school bully, terrifies the local burglars, puzzles the police, and leaves the Dorans' house in an uproar. But there's more to Pin than meets the eye. His best trick is still to come ... £3.99

THE GILTSPUR TRILOGY
Cormac MacRaois
The Battle Below Giltspur, Dance of the Midnight Fire and *Lightning Over Giltspur:* Three exciting tales of adventure and mythology. 'Riveting fantasy ... a fast-moving tale where no words are wasted. From the awakening of the scarecrow Glasán, the story moves at an ever-increasing pace with strange incidents, frightening gatherings and terrifying sequences in rapid succession ... Absolutely brilliant ... exciting, funny and adventurous.' Books Ireland.
£3.99 each, or get all three books in a bright giftpack! £11.99

Classic stories for young readers by John Wood

IN A SECRET PLACE

It was no ordinary trip to the woods for Alice, Yanina, Paul and Benjamin. Yet they never expected to come upon Lord Augustus!

It was an adventure that coloured their lives. And Alice, at least, was determined to return to that secret place, to feel again the magic and half-dream. £3.99

Shortlisted for the Irish Book Awards 1987.

THE W.H.I.F.F. FACTOR!

Audrey Oliphant thinks she has seen it all. McDonalds has had to close, no one can drive, the roads are covered with frogs and it's all because the world has run out of oil while the weather is the wettest ever! Wellies are the most important item you can have so Audrey and her uncle Bernie hatch a plan to recycle all the old wellies they can find with some surprising consequences. A marvellously funny tale that will tickle the fancy of any imaginative reader. £3.99

TROUBLE AT MRS PORTWINE'S

Nominated for the Carnegie Medal. Shortlisted for the Irish Book Awards

Ferdie and Geordie live in a shed. Things might be better if their father didn't have such a passion for sausages ... For one thing, they wouldn't have to steal Mrs Portwine's famous sausages and, in return, spend their nights secretly washing dishes in her café — with unexpected consequences when they become entangled in Samantha's selfish schemes ... £6.95 hardback / £3.99 paperback.

'Imaginative and extremely well-written, it paints in people and places vividly ... a lively and unusual tale.' Irish Times

Available from your bookseller or from
WOLFHOUND PRESS
68 Mountjoy Square, Dublin 1
Tel 01 874 0354. Fax 01 872 0207
Call or write for our catalogue.